THE
RUN OF LIFE

HOW ANY RUNNER CAN REACH
THEIR MOUNTAIN TOP

STEVE TILL

Foreword by London Marathon winner Mike Gratton

Cover image by: Saga, 99 Designs
Book design by: SWATT Books Ltd
Editing and proofreading: Craig Smith (CRS Editorial)

Printed in the United Kingdom
First Printing, 2023

ISBN: 978-1-7394483-0-1 (Paperback)
ISBN: 978-1-7394483-1-8 (eBook)

Still Running
Hampshire, UK

therunoflife.com

For Rod

Thanks for all the grit

Contents

26 Highlights Above and Below 26.2 Miles

2021 500th parkrun

2011 Chicago Marathon
(Completing the set of current Marathon Majors – London, Berlin, New York City, Boston, Chicago)

2003 100th marathon

1996 Represented Great Britain in the European 24-hour Championships

1996 Represented England in the Anglo Celtic Plate 100km (England beat Scotland, Ireland and Wales)

1996 100th running of the Boston Marathon

1995 2nd in National 24-hour Championships

1995 3rd in Compton 40 miles trail race

1994 3rd in National 24-hour Championships

1994 1st in Humberside 24-hour Championships

1994 3rd in National 100km Championships

1989 New York City Marathon

1987 2nd in Solihull 24-hour Championships

1986 1st in Totton Half Marathon

1985 3rd in Southampton Marathon

1985 3rd in Surrey 50 miles Walk (successor to London to Brighton Walk)

1984 Berlin Marathon

1984 5th in Foster's Quadrathon
(2 miles sea swim, 50km race walk, 100 miles cycle, marathon)

1984 2nd in London to Brighton Walk

1983 3rd in London to Brighton Walk

1983 6th in Foster's Quadrathon
(2 miles sea swim, 50km race walk, 100 miles cycle, marathon)

1983   Surrey 100 miles Walk – qualified as Centurion 768 (Have to walk 100 miles in under 24 hours in a judged race)

1982   2nd in London to Brighton Walk

1982   3rd in Bradford 50km Walk

1981   7th in London to Brighton Walk (most famous ultra-distance walk in the world)

1981   1st running of the London Marathon

AN EXAMPLE OF A BUSY RACING SCHEDULE (1984):

1/9   PB at London to Brighton Walk

8/9   Foster's Quadrathon

30/9   PB at Berlin Marathon

7/10   PB at London to Brighton Run

14/10   Winchester Half Marathon

20/10   PB, first sub-60, for 10 miles

28/10   PB at Bedford Marathon

FOREWORD

by Mike Gratton, 1983 London Marathon winner

FOR ME, ONE of the key takeaways from this book is the statement: "Running is not hugely technical, is it?"

This is true, yet so few runners manage to get the best from themselves.

There are so many stories in these pages, most of which I can identify with. One such story is that of the great Rob de Castella of Australia. I ran against 'Deek', as he is known, in the 1982 Commonwealth Games Marathon in Brisbane. As the darling of the home country, he was a kind of pin-up for the Games.

I had qualified as a late selection, as the third marathon member in the England team.

In the Commonwealth race, de Castella was favourite to win – he had run a world marathon best and was the local hero. However, two Tanzanians, Juma Ikangaa, and the returning champion, Gidamis Shahanga, hadn't read the script and took off at a speed well inside Deek's world-best pace.

They opened a sizeable lead over the rest of the chasing pack.

I slipped back off the main group, as I thought it was far too fast – a good move as I did come through late-on to pick up some of the damage done by the early pacemakers, getting to the bronze medal position with a personal best of 2:12:06.

> Author's note: Mike would beat this time the following year – winning the London Marathon in 2:09:43 – and go on to found the runners' travel company, 2:09 Events Limited, later in his career.

De Castella, meantime, was capable of going with the Tanzanians, but it would be a risk. He must have taken another gamble, that they could not hold their pace and would come back to the main group, eventually. Shahanga did in fact drop back, but Ikangaa was not slowing, so in the last 10km de Castella had to dig very deep to close the gap.

He did so, but only to find Ikangaa had the strength to launch another pace attack. Deek reeled him in again, only for the same thing to happen. Third time, de Castella, having caught up again, launched his own attack, the moment he had caught up, this time managing to get away to win.

The pressure de Castella must have been under before the race, the decisions he had to make during it, the toughness when he realised it hadn't gone to plan, and to dig deep into his reserves to rescue the win. Life seldom goes exactly to plan.

As an aside, what happened in the drug testing room after the race revealed the real de Castella.

It was hot, thus the marathon started at 6am. We were in drug testing by 8:30am, before most of the Games village had got up for breakfast. Now, trying to produce a urine sample after a hot marathon could be a long affair. The drug testing team had cold beer to give us – for breakfast. Beer comes in sealed containers, pretty tamper-proof I guess, so it met all our needs.

Deek, with a certain reputation when it came to beer drinking, managed to fill his specimen jar first, and, as he left, called back, "I beat you again, Gratton".

The point of the story is how this simple, technically easy, sport is so complicated in so many other ways.

(By the way, I have learned from reading *The Run of Life* that Rob de Castella and I trained in remarkably similar ways, basically the same pattern each week, which we developed independently on different sides of the world – we had never met until that Brisbane race in 1982.)

I first met Steve Till on a trip to the Swiss Alpine Marathon, a 78km race held in the mountains around Davos. I only ran the 30km support race – doing that as fast as I could was my simple target.

What I learned from ultra-runners like Steve is that they have a different mindset. For them, it's about conquering the distance, no matter how daunting the challenge may be, and therefore about how you think your way through a 78km, 100km or 24-hour race. To do so, they must think differently. It's not dependent entirely on physical ability, as to some extent shorter races are.

It's breaking down the distance into 'mind-coping' chunks, thinking about nutrition on the route, when it is more efficient to walk, not just on steep climbs, how to hold back on long descents to preserve against fatigue in the quads, what to wear, and what to take into the mountains when you can be out for eight hours or more.

Steve really does show that running is a metaphor for life. There are so many ups and downs, so many impossible targets to aim for – getting to run for your country is definitely an accolade that lives with you forever.

Well done, Steve, for putting this simple sport into some context with so many brilliant stories.

PREFACE

LYING ON THE grassy infield[1] of the track in lactic acid agony, having finished last in my school sports day 1,500m, I realised my Olympic dream might be over. The gold medals at 800m and 1,500m that year might just be out of reach!

How could I have come up so short when I had trained so hard? Hadn't I run four-minute miles in my back garden? I was devastated.

It was 1972. I was 14-years-old!

Almost 25 years later, I pulled on a Great Britain vest, realising a dream slightly more realistic than that original delusion. But becoming a British international ultra-runner was a good substitute, and the closest I could get to those Olympic gold medals.

How I got from infield to international is not simple. It involved a lot of hard work, naturally; it required a radical shift of focus; and it depended on a passion for running that saw me participate in, spectate at and cogitate about the sport almost non-stop in the intervening period.

I experienced a lot; I saw a lot; I learnt a lot.

And another 25 years on, I have pored over, mulled over, analysed, sifted and filtered it all sufficiently, that I finally feel able to set down my own

---

1   The infield is the inside of the track, where I simply collapsed upon finishing.

story – and the journeys of others on similar paths – in a way I hope will be useful for, or at least interesting to, you.

Running has given me so much, and if I can support you a little with your own running goals, sporting targets or even life ambitions, then I will feel that I have paid back a bit of what I've received.

The bottom line is I wanted to write a book that any runner, athlete or sportsperson with even the most private, secret, modest objective could pick up and say, "yeah, I've felt like that".

Or, "yeah, that's a good idea, I'll try that".

Or, "oh, I never knew that".

Or, "yeah, that helps".

Whether you run to live, or live to run, however your life runs, you can still have the run of your life.

CHAPTER 1

END – WHERE DO I WANT TO GET TO?

"Summer isn't the time to get too excited about Christmas."

David Hemery (left) and the author, New Hampshire, 1977

IN THE MIDST of his meticulous preparations for the 1968 Mexico City Olympic Games, David Hemery, who would win the 400m hurdles at those Games in a world-record time, was getting bored and frustrated with the relentless training load at his university in the US.

The long runs – eventually covering up to 23 miles in a single day – the weight training, the hills, the interval sessions, all demanded great focus and effort – on top of his already exhausting studies. Rushing from track to lecture hall would sometimes result in agonising cramp at inconvenient moments. He expressed his feelings to his coach, Billy Smith.

Smith urged Hemery to keep his long-term aim in mind, saying: "Summer isn't the time to get too excited about Christmas."[2]

Hemery could see his point and went back to his conditioning with a renewed sense of where he wanted to get to.

But one can understand his momentary loss of perspective and his dismay at the inadequacy of such delayed gratification.

Indeed, how does anyone put in the preparatory work – work that in itself delivers no end result – without keeping the desired outcome firmly and constantly in mind?

Many of us run for fun and fitness – and maybe the occasional parkrun or race – but we perhaps do not finish off a 20-mile run with a 49-second 400m (on a lumpy dirt track at altitude), as Mo Farah did. And he did it because he knew that it was one of the only ways to prepare for the torrid last lap of an Olympic 5,000m final. If he were to achieve his ultimate goal, it had to be done.

Many of us like to sing or play musical instruments, but we perhaps do not practise for eight hours a day as professionals do, because they know that's what their craft, their audience and their pride demands and deserves. As the great Polish pianist Ignacy Jan Paderewski said: "If I miss one day of practice, I notice it. If I miss two days, the critics notice it. If I miss three days, the audience notices it." Again, it had to be done.

---

2   *Another Hurdle*, David Hemery, page 92.

When my wife and I took a year off to travel the world in 1991–1992, we had a lot of time to think. I had already done a lot of running up to that point, but I felt I needed a new target.

Why?

Well, I was ambitious. (Though I saw those teenage Olympic dreams by then to be unrealistic, they still haunted me, bouncing around at the back of my mind.) What **could** I achieve?

I didn't think I could get much faster over the classic 5km, 10km, half marathon and marathon distances – I'd put in the 100-mile weeks, done the speedwork and the long runs, but I seemed to have reached a plateau.

I'd moved on from race walking in 1984, when again I had stopped improving – **and** I had started to get technique problems, causing me to be disqualified on a few occasions.

The headline long trail races like the UTMB (Ultra-Trail du Mont-Blanc) and the Western States 100 hadn't been invented yet.

Triathlon?

Well, despite success in the Quadrathon due to the fortuitous inclusion of a race walk section in the usual swim/bike/run format, sporting stardom there wasn't likely, given I was terrible at swimming (my breaststroke was much faster than my front crawl!) and average at cycling.

So, my mind fixed on to the only real alternative – ultra-running.

Now, I had already run a few of these with some success. Indeed, it seemed that the longer the race went on, the nearer the front I finished: I might come in the 20s or 30s of a local 10km, but in my only 24-hour race up to that point, I had come second – and second to a seasoned international runner at that.

Part of the truth was, of course, that the longer the race, the fewer nutters cared to attempt it. But here perhaps was something that, with proper training, I could be quite successful at. A big fish in an admittedly small pond!

But what would success look like?

Well, it would be nice to set some decent times. It would be great to win or place in some races. And, come to think of it, there were even British and English vests up for grabs, as European and World Championships at 100km and 24 hours (the two globally acknowledged ultra-events) were by now regular occurrences.

An international vest. Representing my country. That would indeed be success.

But I pushed that thought to the back of my mind. There were hundreds of days and thousands of miles to go before I could seriously make that my target.

Life is rarely as binary as sport. But for an ambitious runner, for example, it can be pretty much do or die, life or death, succeed or fail.

In many sports, there is a single achievement that divides the greats from the rest. In tennis or golf, it is winning a Grand Slam or a major. In boxing, it is becoming World Champion. Do you see what I mean?

For athletes at the very top, it's winning Olympic gold or not. It may surprise you that Steve Cram, Paula Radcliffe, Brendan Foster, Liz McColgan and Colin Jackson are just some of those who never did. They had to be content with silvers, bronzes or world records – but were they?

Slightly lower in the pecking order, it's an Olympic medal or no medal; selection for the Olympic team or not; an international vest or not; a four-minute mile or not; making the county team or not; a sub-three-hour marathon or not; a sub-30-minute parkrun or not; a 5km without walking or not. Do you see what I mean? Binary.

At every level, you can see – and you can adopt and accept, if that is your mindset – a clear and quite brutal dividing line between success and failure.

And that's a pretty ruthless way to look at your life.

In most other areas of life, we experience a mixture of success and failure, as well as a lot of bumping along somewhere in the middle. You have a successful career, but maybe you should have got that promotion or won that huge contract. You try and be a good parent, but you only succeed most of the time. If you live in the real world, there are always going to be those "break a window, burn the soufflé, scream the lullaby" moments.[3]

But if you do set yourself such an objective in something as unforgiving as sport, it's black and white.

You don't have to do so, of course, and a lot of people who still take sport seriously don't take such an extreme approach. But, for the 'right' person, it is perhaps a framework that can bring out the best in them.

(A better and more honest word for 'right' might be 'obsessed', 'addicted' or 'nutty'.)

And if it is going to be do or die for that objective, that objective has to be the right objective.

---

3   Quoted from *Coming Around Again* by Carly Simon.

No one's going to die, figuratively speaking, for a goal they don't believe in wholeheartedly.

It would have been silly to stick with my target from when I was 14 and set myself the objective of winning an Olympic gold or running a sub-four-minute mile. Conversely, getting a medal in a local ultra would not really have been enough of a stretch. (I'd already done that anyway, with my second-place 24-hour race.)

But an international vest, wow, that would be fantastic and might just be achievable.

When Roger Bannister ran the first four-minute mile in 1954, he wrote of his feelings on the evening of the race: "My companions were amazed that I could sit so silently, not looking either excited or happy. If only they knew how happy I was! I was resting on billowy white clouds that would, I thought, then, always protect me from the worst of life's buffetings."[4]

That is what I felt about an international vest – whatever else life could have in store for me, whatever failures or frustrations I would encounter, I could always remind myself that I was an international athlete.

It's something that no one would be able to take away. Just as US Presidents are called President for life, international athletes remain so. You can win a 10km or a half marathon, and you are the champion, but if you don't win it again the next year, you lose that status.

But you're always an international athlete.

Indeed, once you have won an international vest, you can legally wear it in any race where you are not representing your club (and therefore should wear that vest).

---

4   *First Four Minutes*, Roger Bannister, pages 193–194.

You can feel the concept of a SMART objective hovering in the background here. The acronym varies between business gurus, but it is generally taken to mean five tests of the validity of a goal – Specific, Measurable, Achievable, Results-orientated and Time-related.

My aim would certainly be specific, measurable and results-orientated. Time didn't matter so much, although I was 35 in 1992, so I didn't have too many years left to do it.

But achievable?

By 1993, I was in the top 20 or so ultra-runners in the UK. With generally four British or English vests available for each championship, I needed to do several things to claim one. I had to work very hard, bring my times down quite a bit, enter all of the relevant races and be sufficiently successful in them…all the while hoping that not too many other young bucks came along in the meantime with the same objective as me!

And what a compelling objective it was.

And that is the main point. It resonated. Without getting too carried away, it sang to my very soul. As soon as I allowed myself to fix upon it, I knew this was something that would drive me on, no matter what.

With that inside me, in my first full winter's training in 1993–1994, after our travels of 1991–1992, I worked very hard.

Ultra-distance running is pretty difficult to prepare yourself for, especially with a full-time job. How can you replicate the feeling of trying to continue to run after 16 hours on the move in a 24-hour race? How can you train yourself to continue to operate at seven or eight-minute miles after 50 miles in a 100km?

I had to earn a living, so I couldn't simply run all day every day – even if that were possible.

I thought long and hard about it, set myself a plan, and I did what I could, committing myself to and completing the crucial sessions that I thought would put me in the best position, to be in with a chance of that vest.

One Bank Holiday weekend saw me run 50 miles on each of the three days.

To prepare for the overnight rigours of a 24-hour race, I would occasionally get up at 2am, run a marathon distance, shower, go back to bed for an hour, then get up again and go to work.

I would also race a marathon and then carry on for a few extra miles.

I would try and run fast marathons only a week apart.

It was important to try and run as hard as I could when I was as tired as I could make myself. So, on my longest training runs, I would sometimes deliberately go all-out for the penultimate hour (so, not the last hour, the second-to-last), condemning myself to an agonising last hour, making that training run far harder, but with far more benefit, I hoped, than a simple long run of that duration.

In other words, I was trying to get the benefit of an eight-hour run from a five-hour one.

On more 'normal' days, my friends would laugh at me for running 10 hard miles in the evening and then just having a cup of coffee and an apple for dinner – and then running another 10 miles the next morning before work.

(I should point out that I only asked my body to do these extreme sessions once it was used to running 100 miles a week hard in the first place.)

I am not telling you all this to make you think what a dedicated chap (or a nutter) I was, but to prove my assertion that, if you identify the right target – the one that resonates with your passion – then motivation is not a problem.

And so, the point is, there was never any doubt in my mind about whether I was going to run any of those sessions. Like Mo Farah's last 400m, or Paderewski's hours of practice, they had to be done.

The objective – the prize that I felt I might get – was too compelling for me not to.

People say you can do anything you want to, if you really put your mind to it. Certainly, it was my mind and soul, not my body, that called for me to go out on all those mighty excursions. My body wanted to turn over and go back to sleep. It was my mind and my spirit that could see the prize.

So, I would amend the saying, "You can do anything you want to, if you put your mind to it."

I would say (certainly in a sporting context): "If you can choose the target that is just about achievable, that is right on the outer edge of your potential, and that speaks to your soul, and if you can decide in your mind what you need to do to achieve it, and if you then give your body the chance to grow, to develop and to adapt to it, then you can indeed achieve whatever your soul's wisdom has fixed upon."

So, I did the training, I did the races and I did the times, so that by early 1996, I was in contention.

The Chief Selector of the Great Britain and Northern Ireland ultra-running team asked me to prove my fitness and form for that autumn's European 24-hour Championships in Courçon, France. We both felt that a full 24-hour race before then would be too much, so he asked me to run a 12-hour trial.

"Try and reach 80 miles," he said.

There it was – simple, stark, binary. Run 80 miles in 12 hours – basically, three consecutive sub-four-hour marathons – and the long-coveted vest would be mine.

So, in the absence of an actual 12-hour race, I went up to Doncaster to a 24-hour race and ran round and round the 400m cinder track.

It went OK to start with. I reached 100km (62.1 miles) in just under nine hours. At that point, if you work it out, I just needed to maintain 10-minute miles for the next three hours to fulfil his request and secure my international place.

Just!!

I ploughed on. At one point, with about 90 minutes to go, I found myself slipping outside the required pace. With everything on the line, I focused even harder ("Come ON!") and upped my speed to run nearly 80.5 miles in the allotted time.

A couple of months later, I was pulling on a British vest.

What would be your equivalent of winning that vest?

By the way, when I finally received my call-up for Great Britain and Northern Ireland for the 1996 European 24-hour Championships, the men's team consisted of James Zarei, one of the two or three people to have run over 1,000km (621 miles) in six days, Richard Brown, who held the LEJOG (Land's End to John O'Groats) record, Don Ritchie, generally recognised as the greatest ultra-runner of all time…and me! Company like that will give you imposter syndrome – that voice in your head that says, "You don't deserve to be here".

But I knew how hard I'd worked, and I knew what I'd achieved.

Up to that point, only two men had ever won medals in both ultra-distance national championships (100km, 24 hours) in the same year – Don Ritchie and me! So, I guess it depends how you slice the data! Deep down, I knew I deserved my vest.

(Again, that voice can chime in: "But you only scraped two bronzes in 1994, while Don got multiple golds. You can't compare yourself!")

Unless you are Mo Farah in 2012, Don Ritchie in 1978, Paula Radcliffe in 2003, or Usain Bolt in 2012, there will always be someone better than you, and always someone worse than you. Don't let your pride be an excuse not to try.

CHAPTER 2
DEEP – WHY AM I DOING THIS?

"You know that they laugh at how slow you are?"

Bristol University Cross Country Club 1976, the author is second right

PAULA RADCLIFFE FINISHED 299th in her first cross-country race, but she persisted because she had a passion. Mamo Wolde competed for Ethiopia at 800m, 1,500m and the 4 x 400m relay at his first Olympic Games in 1956. It's fair to say he took his time to discover his best event, but eventually won Olympic gold in the marathon in 1968!

At university, I loved running. I would train twice a day – but I didn't seem to improve. When I was in my second year, a first-year student with whom I was friendly joined the cross-country club and later said to me: "You know that the rest of the team laugh at you for how much you train but how slowly you run?"

I was a bit put out, but it didn't go too deep. It didn't kill the passion.

I can see now that, really, I had no or little physical talent for running, and that it would take more than a year or so of consistent training for my hard work to offset my poor genes. The talent I did possess was more in my heart and my head, than in my legs. I had the passion and the belief to push and to persist.

Passion can take you a long way. My point here is that you don't have to possess great talent to achieve great things. You only have to look at a handful of successes at the 2020 (actually, 2021) Tokyo Olympic Games to see what can be achieved, and more importantly what can be overcome. Even at this elite level, perhaps some of what these guys had was talent, but certainly what they all shared was passion – and persistence.

Let's start with Tom Daley's situation in 2021.

The Chinese pair stood on the 10m platform. They needed 102 points from their final dive to win gold – and deprive our hero of the top step on the podium. They took off, tumbling through their complex sequence of somersaults and twists. It looked good, very good. Then came the agonising wait for the judges' verdict.

The scoreboards blinked into life – they had managed 101.52 and so the gold medals in the synchronised 10m platform diving went to Daley and Matty Lee.

After coming seventh and eighth at the Beijing 2008 Games, winning a bronze and a fourth place in London 2012, and a bronze and an 18th place in Rio 2016, Tom Daley had finally won an Olympic gold medal.

Going further back in his career, of course, there were the years of early morning training sessions, of family sacrifice, and even in 2016, after the disappointment of another gold-less games, Tom had to be convinced to carry on in the sport by his husband and other close family.

(He backed up his gold in Tokyo with a bronze in the 10m individual – and some impressive knitting!)

Equestrian team-eventer Laura Collett fought back from an unkind past. She suffered a heavy fall from her horse in 2013, having to be resuscitated five times, with paramedics giving her an emergency tracheotomy. She sustained a fractured shoulder, a punctured lung, broken ribs, a lacerated liver and kidney damage. A bone fragment from her shoulder detached and travelled through her blood stream to her right eye, damaging her optic nerve. She was placed in an artificially induced coma for six days.

Her career had started so promisingly, too, with Laura winning numerous significant medals, including the supreme pony title at the 2003 Horse of the Year Show, when she was just 13.

But she didn't give up after the accident. She got back on that horse – figuratively and literally – and in Tokyo, Laura won the Team Eventing gold medal with Oliver Townend and Tom McEwen.

In the London 2012 triathlon, Jonny Brownlee was given a 15-second time penalty for riding his bike before the transition zone, and so had to sit for that length of time during the run, ending up claiming the bronze medal behind his brother, Alistair, and Javier Gómez of Spain.

Jonny collapsed with heatstroke upon finishing but suffered no lasting harm.

At the Rio 2016 Olympic Games, the brothers won gold and silver, with Alistair again on top of the podium.

Finally, in Tokyo, in the inaugural Mixed Relay event, Jonny teamed up with Jessica Learmonth, Georgia Taylor-Brown and Alex Yee, to win gold.

Years of competing with his brother in their arduous training sessions, including agonising runs over the West Yorkshire hills, had finally paid off, with Jonny becoming the most successful Olympic triathlete of all time – the only one with three medals.

Across the Pennines in Lancashire, Holly Bradshaw may not be as much of a household name, but her profile should be higher, given she regularly reaches the altitude of a double-decker bus with her pole vaulting.

Her consistency had won her many minor medals and taken her to the finals of numerous global competitions – only for that much sought-after podium position to elude her in the end. Sixth in London 2012, she was seventh in the 2015 World Championships, fifth at the Rio 2016 Games, sixth in the 2017 World Championships and fourth in the same championships of 2019.

Then came Tokyo.

Apart from the running, the weights, the gymnastics, the stretching and the vaulting, she had also prepared for the literal heat of the competition in Japan, by sitting in a hot tub for 25 minutes at 41 degrees, with just her head sticking out of the water and a thermometer in her ear!

In a very tight final, Holly won bronze, vaulting 4.85m, with the gold being won at 4.90m.

James Guy won Sports Personality of Warrington when he was quite young. At the presentation ceremony, the compere asked him what training he did, and James told him that, three mornings a week, he got up at 4am, ate his breakfast in the car, swam for two hours and then went to school. There were gasps from the audience. You see, James was 11-years-old at the time.

In swimming terms, this Guy had been around forever. In a sport where you generally retire in your early twenties, James had hung on in there until 2021 to try and win the Olympic gold that had eluded him.

After all the sacrifices, winning silver on relay teams at the Rio 2016 Olympic Games was not really enough, and in Tokyo – the 4am starts, the endless lengths of the pool, all the land-based training, the family taxi service, the non-existent social life, the shaving down – all of it suddenly became worthwhile as he claimed not one but two Olympic gold medals.

He partnered with Tom Dean, Duncan Scott, Matthew Richards and Calum Jarvis to win the 4 x 200m freestyle relay, and with Adam Peaty, Anna Hopkin, Kathleen Dawson and Freya Anderson to claim gold in the inaugural mixed medley relay.

And Laura Muir!

Like Bradshaw, Muir had won medals – the European golds, outdoors and in, and silver and bronze at the World Indoor Championships. But in global outdoor finals, she had finished fifth at the World Championships in 2015, seventh at the Rio 2016 Games, fourth in the 1,500m and sixth in the 5,000m at the 2017 World Championships in London, and fifth at the World Championships in 2019.

Having set a personal best at 800m in 2021, and qualified for an Olympic place in that event, she relinquished it to focus exclusively on the 1,500m. By contrast, one of her main rivals, Sifan Hassan, the Ethiopia-born Dutchwoman, decided to try the unprecedented 1,500m, 5,000m and 10,000m treble.

Laura ran a perfect tactical race. She was always going to find it very difficult to beat the defending champion, Faith Kipyegon of Kenya, but she got away from the rest of the field in the last lap with just Kipyegon and Hassan, overtook the latter on the last bend, and ran for all she was worth to claim a wonderful silver medal.

(Sifan Hassan did win the 5,000m and 10,000m though!)

Athletes, swimmers, triathletes, divers and horse riders tend to flash across our screens once every four years at Olympics time! This can lead us to get the impression that they are overnight successes – just turning up on the day and winning medals.

David Hemery tells the story of a small boy approaching him and saying: "My Dad says you don't have to train. It's just natural." This must have been a bit galling, given that Hemery had just completed the 500th press-up and 500th sit-up of his pre- pre-season session![5]

Every competitor at the Tokyo 2020 Olympic Games – and in every other major sporting arena – will have a story to tell about their journey to get there. Some of them will be short stories, like that of 13-year-old bronze-medallist skateboarder Sky Brown, and some will be longer, like 51-year-old Spanish race walker Jesús Ángel García, who was competing in his eighth Olympic Games.

And one senses that, in most cases, it has all been worth it. Whether it's finally clinching an Olympic gold medal – Tom Daley, Laura Collett, Jonny Brownlee and James Guy – or a global medal – Holly Bradshaw and Laura Muir – or whether it's someone simply fulfilling a destiny, their rightful place in their chosen sport, they all knew why they were doing it – and why they were still trying to reach beyond the obstacles of injuries, setbacks, frustrations, failures and, in the case of Jonny Brownlee, an annoying older brother!

However different their sports, their stories and their journeys, one thing they do all share is a passion for what they do, which gives them the persistence to keep going.

---

5   *Another Hurdle*, David Hemery, page 97.

Another way of looking at this subject – basically of nature versus nurture, how much of sporting success is down to talent and how much to hard work – is to consider Lottery funding. Since Lottery funding was introduced, British success at the Olympic Games has been transformed.

But what does Lottery funding do? Well, one thing it doesn't do is change athletes' genetic make-up – their DNA. What it **does** do is allow those with enough talent, commitment, dedication and so on, the vital access to the best coaches, psychologists, nutritionists, massage therapists, etc. A prime example would be giving the cycling squad access to Chris Boardman's celebrated 'marginal gains'. And perhaps even more importantly, it gives those sportspeople time to train and time to recover between training.

So, given that, in 1996, Great Britain and Northern Ireland won one gold medal at the summer Olympics, coming 36th on the unofficial medals table, and that in the last three Games we've amassed 29, 27 and 22 golds, coming third, second and fourth, maybe nurture is more of a deciding factor than nature.

Now, you and I may not be able to aspire to Olympic competition, but we all have goals within us. If we are truthful with ourselves, we know there is a target nagging away at the back of our minds. Given the above supposition that a lot of hard work can overcome a lot of shortcomings in natural ability, we shouldn't sell ourselves short by setting too low a bar for our ambition.

We have to appreciate that no one is an overnight success, and that the depth of our feeling of satisfaction upon the successful achievement of our target is directly proportional to the effort, the sacrifice and the time it took to get there.

If our target is the right one, then our passion for it can carry us through.

What is your target?

Where is your passion?

CHAPTER 3

HELP – WHY AM I WRITING THIS BOOK?

"You can do better than this."

The England 100km squad for the 1996 Anglo Celtic Plate, with the author far right

I REALLY WANTED to call this book, 'Everything I know about life, I've learnt from running', but, while tempting, it wouldn't be completely accurate.

As I said in the Preface, running has taught me many lessons, most of which are common sense, but which I hope you will nonetheless find useful. If nothing else, this book is stuffed full of stories about runners and other sportspeople, gathered from my 50-odd years of watching, coaching, training and competing, and I hope that, if the more explicit of my advice doesn't hit home for you ("do this!"), then these stories will perhaps provide some more subtle, circuitous inspiration – via the back door, as it were ("they did this – and it worked!").

But why me? Why have I got the nerve, the arrogance, to set myself up as this running guru, who can tell you all the secrets and give you all the answers?

Well, obviously, I'm not a running guru.

I've never been on an Olympic team or won major medals. I'm no Mo or Paula.

But I have won national championships and I've worn the vest of my country. I have spent more than 50 years battling to be the best I could be at road running, cross-country, trail running, track running, triathlon, race walking and ultra-running.

In addition to international vests, I have run more than 100 marathons, more than 500 parkruns and qualified as a Centurion for race walking 100 miles in less than 24 hours in a judged race.

I have also completed two Ironman-plus triathlons – actually, Quadrathons, consisting of a two-mile sea swim, 50km race walk, 100-mile cycle and marathon.

I have completed all of the Marathon Majors, as they were when I could run a marathon (London in 1981, Berlin in 1984, New York City in 1989, Boston in 1996 and Chicago in 2011).

And I've done some of the most iconic races – the London to Brighton (the Walk and the Run versions), the Barry 40-mile track race, the South London Harriers 30, the South Downs Way 80, the Swiss Alpine Marathon.

(I still beat myself up for not doing races such as the West Highland Way, the Comrades Marathon, Western States 100 and the Athens Marathon. But you can't do everything and, to be fair, in my peak years when tackling those would have been possible, I was busy completing the races I needed to do, to be considered for the English and British ultra-distance teams.)

So, I've done practically the widest possible range of endurance events, each to a reasonably high standard, across many years.

I've also coached dozens of runners of all standards, and spectated at numerous events – from local to international, from parkrun to the Olympic Games. Ultimately, I'm an athletics fan as well as a participant, and I have thought ceaselessly and written extensively about this simple but endlessly fascinating sport.

I am old enough, for instance, to have been at Crystal Palace in 1973, shouting Brendan Foster on to a two-mile world record, shaving 0.2 seconds off Lasse Virén's time!

And perhaps more importantly than all this, unlike Mo and Paula, I'm just an ordinary runner. As my university cross-country teammates knew all too well, I had little or no talent for running. So I had to do what I did on my own, with no sponsorship, and whilst holding down a job and bringing up a family.

So, I guess what I'm trying to say is that, unless you **are** Mo Farah or Paula Radcliffe reading this book (hi, a bit of a mention on social media would be very welcome, thank you!), I am more like you, dear reader, than they are.

I hope that my story, my viewpoint on life and sport, can speak to you, whatever your starting point, whatever your standard and whatever your aim.

Running has given me such joy. And that joy is derived from success – the satisfaction of aiming for something you're not sure is achievable and achieving it. And that success is a result of the passion. And the passion defines the target.

OK?

I'll go over that again!

So, first you identify where your passion lies. That determines what your target should be – a target that is almost out of reach, but which resonates with your passion. Then you have to think carefully about what you need to do to achieve that target. Then you put in the hard work. With a little bit of luck, you achieve that target – which means success, satisfaction and joy.

We really ought to have a diagram!

It would be great therefore for this book to communicate that passion and that joy to you, and so to help you define your own passion – the passion that can bring you satisfaction and success – and ultimately enjoyment.

I am reminded of Ron Daws. Daws isn't a household name, but he represented USA in the marathon at the 1968 Mexico City Olympic Games. Daws called himself the 'Self-Made Olympian', indeed that was the title of the book he wrote about his career.

Like me, Daws felt that he had little or no talent as a runner, but just dedicated himself to being the best he could possibly be, and that resulted in his berth on the Olympic team.

"Unless you go all out for something," he said, "you may conclude your life without actually having lived it.

"It doesn't have to be running, but it should be a quest for excellence, and it need be for only that period of your life that it takes to fully explore it. That's how you find out what you are made of. That's how you find out who you are. To live your life your way, to reach for the goals you have set for yourself, to be 'the you' that you want to be, that is success."[6]

The American novelist, Jack London (1876–1916, author of *The Call of the Wild* and *White Fang*), put it rather more poetically: "I would rather be ashes than dust! I would rather that spark should burn out in a brilliant blaze than it should be stilled by dry rot. I would rather be a superb meteor, every atom of me in magnificent glow, than a sleepy and permanent planet. The proper function of man is to live, not to exist. I shall not waste my days trying to prolong them. I shall use my time."[7]

Now it's all very well for me to load you down with these quotes about giving your all, laying it all on the line, doing your absolute best…

I remember my mother saying to me before every school exam or test, "Just do your best. That's all we ask."

My best! My absolute best! Do you really know what you're asking?

You're asking me to screw every last ounce of effort and knowledge out of myself in those hours in the exam hall or those minutes in the classroom. Do you actually know how difficult that is?

---

6   As quoted by Joe Henderson, *Runner's World*, December 1992, page 14.

7   As quoted by Tom Jordan, *Pre*, back cover.

In the same way, it's all very well me repeating these marvellous, supposedly inspiring exhortations to you; it's quite another thing for you to pour a lifetime's commitment into the quest.

How do you do it?

First, as I have said, you need the right quest.

One of Ron Daws's mantras was: "You can do better than this."[8]

He questioned and probed any received wisdom he came across, and he refined it for his own purposes. He experimented with training systems, and he felt the success that he had was down to harnessing every possible benefit.

He was tough on himself, and on others. Indeed, as a running coach, he was only as hard on others as he had been on himself countless times.

He died suddenly from a heart attack at the age of 55 on 28th July 1992.

Four days later, on the other side of the world, the women's Olympic marathon was taking place in Barcelona. Lorraine Moller of New Zealand, who had once been married to Daws, was 37-years-old and not predicted to make any impact in the race.

Indeed, she did not figure in the early going, but eventually she moved up to claim a hugely unexpected bronze medal.

---

8   As quoted by Joe Henderson, *Runner's World*, December 1992, page 14.

I am not the first romantic old fool to wonder if, somewhere in those middle miles, when she was trailing some distance behind the medal positions, she didn't hear Ron Daws's voice inside her head repeating the mantra: "You can do better than this."

And she did.

And so can you.

Can you do better than this?

And can this book help you?

CHAPTER 4
COMMIT – WHY AM I HESITATING?

"Get on with it!"

THE THREE RUNNERS I was coaching for the London Marathon met at my house for a long run. After the traditional faffing session, involving an intricate choreography of them each needing to attend in turn to drinks, shoelaces, Vaseline®, Strava, layers and the loo…finally, miraculously, all three were simultaneously ready to start.

I showed them (shoved them?) out of the door, reassuring them that I'd see them in a few miles with drinks.

They went out of the gate and began walking along the road, still chatting.

I leaned out of the kitchen window. "Get on with it!" I shouted.

Of course, beneath the coach's bluster, I did sympathise. I'd done it a million times myself. When you're about to start a hard session – whether it's a long run, a hill session or some speedwork – what's the last thing you feel like doing? The hard session, of course.

And the body and mind conspire with this feeling, don't they?

How many times have you woken up on the day of a crucial workout with a sore knee or a bit of a sniffle, or just the overriding thought that you've got to clean that oven before you go out.

It's psychosomatic. It's hypochondria. It's human nature.

Even Matthew Pinsent (four Olympic golds) prayed for the vehicle he was travelling in on the way to his rowing finals, to be involved in an accident ("I could be loaded into an ambulance, smiling."[9]) to save him from the agony of the test.

Of course, when you start out on some sporting quest, trepidation is a problem.

But willpower is like a muscle. You train it and it becomes stronger.

Emil Zátopek, Czech winner of four Olympic gold medals, said: "If one can stick to the training throughout many long years, then willpower is no longer a problem. It's raining? That doesn't matter. I am tired? That's besides the point. It's simply that I just have to."

---

9   *A Lifetime in a Race*, Matthew Pinsent, page 319.

That's why I tell everybody to keep a training diary, preferably one that lets you see a week at a glance. Because, once you get beyond the perilous first few weeks, and you can look back and see that you've, say, run three times a week for four weeks, if you are reluctant to go out one day, sight of that diary is likely to evoke the thought: "Hmm, I've come this far. I can't stop now. Maybe I will just go out and see if this knee gets better, the sniffle goes away, and the oven cleans itself."

Wherever you are – whether you know what your target is, or you're just starting out and figuring it out – getting going and keeping going is difficult. Even David Hemery found it so.

But what gets the ambitious athlete who has just found their goal, the improver who has never really thought about it before but is now starting to think, or the beginner who nevertheless has a passion for what they've just discovered, out of the door, is that target.

Or a coach shouting: "Get on with it!"

As I have said, what really gets you out of the door is the right target, the target for which you have passion.

I can't decide what that means for you.

Only you will know that, if, when someone says, "Could you represent Essex at cross-country?" no light bulb goes on in your heart, soul and mind, but when someone says, "Could you get a county medal?" it does.

"Could you make the county hockey squad?"

"Could you break into the first team?"

"Could you break two hours for the half marathon?"

You have to tune into your passion.

People say to me, "I hate running". Great, well don't effing run then. You've got to find where your passion is leading you, for it will surely lead you towards your target.

It took me a few years to find the right one.

Lying on that grassy infield, having finished last in my school sports day 1,500m, I did indeed think that my Olympic dream might be over (see Preface).

You see, I loved running, and I was desperate to be good at it. I was inspired by the courage of David Bedford of Great Britain and Northern Ireland, who had led for 24 of the 25 laps of the 1971 European 10,000m in Helsinki.

And I was mesmerised by the speed of Juha Väätainen of Finland and Jürgen Haase of East Germany, who each ran the last 400m of that race in 53 seconds. Looking like a 100m sprinter, the Finn eventually prevailed in front of his ecstatic home crowd (Bedford ended up sixth).

Determined to be like them, I would go out at night and run round our garden, avoiding the washing line, zigzagging across the patio and ducking under the trees. I reckoned it was about 30 laps to a mile, and I calculated I was getting very close to four minutes!

Carry on like this, I thought, and it would be at least one gold medal, maybe two, later that year at the Munich Olympic Games.

It was 1972. I was 14-years-old.

Let's back up a year or so.

It was all Pelé's fault really. Well, him and Jairzinho, Gérson, Tostão, Rivellino, Carlos Alberto and all the rest of the great Brazilian World Cup winning side of 1970.

Back then, I was football mad. I just about remembered the previous World Cup, and the 1970 England side were supposed to be even better than the 1966 winning team. But we were beaten 3–2 by West Germany in the quarter-finals; they then lost 4–3 to Italy in the semis; and then the Italians lost 4–1 to Brazil in the final.

The whole tournament was amazing, but Pelé was its star – shooting from his own half, selling Ladislao Mazurkiewicz, the Uruguay goalkeeper, an outrageous dummy on the edge of the penalty area, bringing **that** save out of Gordon Banks in the group match, laying off a glorious pass for Carlos Alberto to score the last goal of the final.

I loved it. Trouble was, a couple of months later, when the English football season resumed, West Brom versus Millwall just didn't cut it. What an anti-climax. Pelé had spoilt it all for me. Football would never mean as much to me again.

Into this sudden vacuum of sports fandom rushed athletics. David Bedford was setting records; David Hemery, Olympic 400m hurdles champion in 1968, was still running; people like Brendan Foster and Alan Pascoe were emerging; and on the evening of 10th August 1971, Bedford and Väätainen changed my life forever.

After watching that race, I did not know what to do. I just sat there.

Then I did the only thing that made any sense. I went outside and ran up and down the long, steep hill where we lived.

You see, I was just trying to connect with those athletes, to be part of their world of athleticism and pain. I was desperate to join in the same activity and – although obviously nowhere near as fast – like them, I was running, and, like them, I was trying to run as fast as possible when tired.

After running up and down that hill a few times, I felt that the gap between them and me, which had been vast at the beginning, was a tiny bit narrower.

To be honest, I've been trying to narrow it ever since.

I kept on training into the next year – training pretty hard, I thought, with qualifying for the 1972 Munich Olympics very much in mind. Those four-minute miles in the back garden surely made me the pre-race favourite!

So, you can see that the sports day 1,500m failure came as a bit of a shock.

How could I try so hard and come up so short? How could I train so much and achieve so little?

Well, I kept on running, and the next year at sports day, I was second instead of last. But I was desperate to find an athletics endeavour at which I could succeed. I tried decathlon. I tried race walking.

I ploughed on at university, coming near the back of the cross-country field on a weekly basis. I remember being out of sight of any other runner in one wintry competition, and slipping over on the ice. I lay there for what seemed like ages, trying to find my glasses in the snow, assuming I was last. I wasn't. There was a runner behind me, and his name was Winterbottom, although it was my glutes that were in close proximity to the seasonal freeze!

I remember when I took up race walking after university, I vowed with the chutzpah of youth that, if I ever came last in a race, I'd give up. A couple of weeks later, a 3,000m race at Crystal Palace produced a classier field than

I had anticipated. Still, I was comfortably ahead of the only man behind me with a lap to go…until he produced a sprint finish I could not match. My personal best was no consolation.

But I didn't give up, and gradually things improved. It's amazing what a bit of hard training can do.

My times plummeted and my results soared. I even won a few local races.

But it wasn't until I turned my attention to ultra-distance running that things really took off. National medals and that call-up to the British team eventually followed.

That was in 1996, a full quarter of a century on from the race that originally inspired me.

And I never forgot my 1972 school sports day, a bitter memory that made any success all the sweeter.

Now, I am not saying that everyone can go from last to first, but as long as you 'last' at something, you won't be last in the end.

My main point is this: it may not be immediately obvious what your true target should be. In 1971–1972, mine was to win gold medals at Olympic middle-distance events. Cruel reality showed me the folly of that, of my quest for Olympic decathlon gold (Daley Thompson was, I had to admit, a bit more talented than I was!) and for race walking supremacy.

But, eventually, I knew that ultra-running was the right arena and a more realistic target, one around which my passion rallied.

Where is your passion taking you?

CHAPTER 5

DO – WHAT SHOULD I DO?

"That is very slow. You must run harder."

OVER THE YEARS, many top runners have been asked how they train and, as a follow-up, what their interlocutor could do to improve their own running. I remember watching a Kenyan athlete, who had run about 12:50 for 5,000m, being asked by a fan (who had run about 16 minutes) what to do.

"Sixteen minutes?" said the Kenyan. "That is very slow. You must run harder."

"Just run harder?"

"Yes, run harder."

I also remember a British ultra-distance runner winning a 100km race in France and being asked about their secret to training for these very long efforts.

"Get lost," he said, a comment that was misinterpreted at the time, but what he meant was that he deliberately ran until he didn't know where he was – in order to have to run further to find his way back home!

What you actually do, of course, depends on your target, and I cannot possibly cover here every scenario for every sportsperson or every runner. When I first sit down with someone I am going to coach, we have a lengthy conversation – not just about their past and present exercise routine and their future goals, but also about any other parameters – factors that will influence the advice I give and the schedule I set.

Someone with a demanding, manual job will find it difficult to run twice a day. Someone with a young family may have to do all of their training very early in the morning. Someone who travels a lot with work will find it difficult to stick to a regular weekly routine.

I am reminded of Derek Turnbull, the New Zealand sheep farmer, who at one time held every masters (veterans) world record for his age group, from 800m to the marathon. The training he could manage, and the races he could enter, revolved around life on the farm. At lambing time, he did no running at all.

A rival of his, who worked at a desk all day, commented that the hardest thing he himself did was go for a 10-mile run...and the easiest thing Derek did all day was go for a 10-mile run!

I stayed on Derek's farm twice in the 1990s (he died in 2006 at the age of 79) and ran with him – well, mostly someway behind him. He was certainly a character, one of his sayings being: "No socks, no watches, no stretching."

I was a decent runner at the time (maybe around 34 minutes for 10km) but he took me on an eight-mile run and, with about two miles to go, he said: "I like to muck around a bit from here."

And with that he left me struggling along, still running somewhere near six-minute miles, while he took hundreds of yards out of me in running close to five-minute miles.

This was in December 1991. Four months later, in London, he set the then world record for an over-65-year-old of 2:41:57.

And that was off a training programme that was patchy, to say the least.

When a runner stayed at his farmhouse B&B, he'd do a bit more. When John Campbell (then masters world record holder in the marathon) was in town, he'd do a bit more. When there was a race coming up, he'd do a bit more. He had raced himself fit before London by clocking six masters' world records (800m, 1,500m, one mile, 3,000m, 5,000m, 10,000m) in New Zealand in the month before the marathon.

He could get away with it.

We can't!

So, what you actually do will depend on your target – and the time and energy available to you.

As I say, I can't give you all a schedule – not until we've sat down together – but I can refer you to my own example of thinking very carefully about how I would fit training for ultra-distance running into my life.

For races like the 100km lasting, for me, 7–8 hours (OK – mostly 8–9!), and the 24 hours lasting, well, 24 hours, the 'usual' runner's diet of up to an hour during the week and a two-hour run on Sunday mornings, isn't going to cut it. So one needs to be creative.

The Bank Holiday weekend was an excellent opportunity to maximise mileage with those three 50-mile runs. Using the working day as a deadline gave me the idea of getting up very early and fitting in the marathon distance run at 2am. That wasn't just for the physical benefit, of course. It was for the mental boost of knowing that no one else would think of doing this! Of course, they might, but I was pretty confident I was in a class of very few.

Otherwise, I had to look for ways to make the training as hard as possible. Running 10 miles wasn't hard for me then, but running 10 miles hard at night, then just having an apple and a coffee (plus water) for dinner, and then getting up in the morning and running another 10 was certainly demanding. It was a way of being creative, of getting more out of my training for the same amount of time and distance.

A better return on my investment, if you like.

And that is what I would encourage everyone to do, especially if you have a tough job and a demanding family – or a tough family and a demanding job!

Could you speed up towards the end of a long run to increase its value? (For instance, I always encourage any runner training for a marathon to run two-thirds to three-quarters of their long runs at a manageable pace, and then perhaps on some runs speed up by 30–60 seconds a mile for the last 3–4 miles.) Could you double the benefit of your gym session by running there and back?

Could you, as I did, deliberately blast the penultimate hour of a very long run, to make the last hour as testing as possible, replicating the fatigue one would normally encounter on a much longer effort? Could you enhance the effect of a speed session by cutting the recovery between the last few reps?

Brendan Foster won the 1974 European 5,000m by injecting a 59-second lap with five circuits to go. His crucial session in preparing for this – and proving he could pull it off, that it was worth attempting – was a series of very fast 200m efforts, with only 30 seconds between. Completing these sessions taught him that he could indeed kick in the middle of a race and not get into debilitating oxygen debt. Wanting to maximise the value of that session, Foster would often cut the recovery between the last couple of reps down to little more than 20 seconds!

Again, more bang for his buck.

David Hemery, again, trained through the winter of Boston, USA, in preparation for the 1968 Olympic Games. Every other athlete at the university was on the indoor track completing their sessions under the heated dome. Hemery arrived one freezing afternoon, expecting his coach to cancel the scheduled outdoor session of reps on the snow-covered track.

The athlete asked if he should do some weights or just rest. But Billy Smith pushed his shoulder against the door and said: "Out there is the road to Mexico."[10]

Having said that, probably **that** you do (something) is more important than **what** you do. And for that, you need a process.

I just said that it was impossible to give every runner a schedule, here in this book, but let me push the debate along a little bit by saying that, in very general terms, there are normally three key sessions in each week.

---

10 *Another Hurdle*, David Hemery, page 23.

Let's start at the very top.

"That was harder than it looked," said Steve Ovett, after 'the most casual finishing kick imaginable' (last 200m in 27.2) had taken him to the Southern 3,000m championship title in 1978. He explained: "I ran five miles this morning and a hard '10' at midday."[11] He then finished his day's work with a session of 60m sprints!

The preternaturally gifted Ovett (Olympic 800m gold, European 1,500m gold, Commonwealth 5,000m gold, occasionally also winning 200s and half marathons!) could get away with working all of his 'gears' – from endurance through speed-endurance to sheer speed – in one day. We probably can't.

In setting schedules for my athletes who are seeking to go faster at 5km, 10km and half marathon, I emphasise three key sessions that address their different needs in each seven days.

(This assumes that the athlete in question has done the requisite build-up, is generally used to running five or six times a week for up to an hour, and is ambitious and prepared to work hard.)

Sunday is an obvious choice for the longer run, which would increase, week by week, from the athlete's longest run in the recent past, culminating in around 5–6 miles for our 5km wannabe, 8–9 miles for the 10km aspirant, and 11 miles for the 'half' hopeful. Over-distance work is necessary for the first two, whilst 11 miles is sufficient for the 13.1-mile test of the half marathon.

Pace for these runs is less important than for the other sessions, but, as a coach, I would like to see the 'half' runner, for example, hitting speeds

---

11 As reported by *Athletics Weekly*, 27th May 1978, page 8.

around a minute a mile slower than their target pace, towards the end of the build-up.

The other two key sessions would be undertaken on Tuesdays and Thursdays, leaving the rest of the week clear for easy running, gym sessions and even a relaxed parkrun on Saturdays, as long as it did not compromise the freshness required for the following day's outing.

Tuesdays would be tempo runs – in my opinion, the most important session of the week. This work is designed to raise the cruising speed to the required level.

So, one of my athletes was determined to take her half marathon personal best from 2:11 (almost exactly 10-minute miles) to under two hours – a tall order. Initially, she could just about run a tempo effort at 10-minute miles for four miles.

We built up from three separate miles at 9:30, to two continuous miles at 9, then three separate miles at 8:30, and so on, eventually reaching four miles non-stop at 8:30 – indicative, in a training context, of an ability to hold 9s for around the required time! We were inching her, week by week, towards the required pace.

We knew that it was essential, in a 13.1-mile race, for her to feel that the required 9:00 pace was easy-ish in the initial miles, doable (with focus) in the middle section, and still within her determined compass towards the end.

At the other end of the scale, a 21:00 5km runner aiming for a sub-20-minute time might start being able to hold a 7:00 pace for a mile in training, but we would build-up through half miles at a 6:30 pace (i.e. 3:15 for 800m), then a 6:00 pace, to separate miles at those paces, before attempting a mile, then a mile-and-a-half at 6:20 – the target speed. Sustained speed at the target pace – these sessions ain't easy!

The Thursday sessions would work the higher gears – the sheer speed and leg strength required – alternating between flat efforts with limited recovery – perhaps 6–10 efforts of 30–60 seconds at 90% of maximum, and the same jog recovery – and hill sprints, again near-maximum efforts of 6–10 times 30–60 seconds up a medium incline, with a strict jog-down recovery.

This is the sort of session that sees me standing at the bottom of the hill, whistle round neck, stopwatch in hand, shouting things like, "Turn straight round, don't dawdle at the top," and, somewhere in the middle reps, "Don't leave it all for the last effort – anyone can do that – commit now!"

The tempo and speed/hill sessions, of course, demand a thorough warm-up of jogging and strides, and a lovely, mellow, "Thank God that's over!" warm-down jog at the end.

My athletes and I believe that the long runs provide the necessary endurance to maintain the required pace over the whole distance, and that, at the other end of the scale, the hills and flat efforts supply the leg strength and raw speed to make that pace feel easier (at least at first), and that the tempo sessions work directly in the crucial pace zones, moving the athlete from where they are (holding 10-minute miles for four miles, say), to where they need to be (8:30-minute miles for the same distance).

Training seriously for an event has to be multi-layered, in this way. It is about working on all of your 'gears' in the different sessions, so that, on race day, the speed, strength, speed-endurance and sheer stamina all come together to give the athlete the best possible opportunity to deliver an optimum performance.

Ovett could basically work on all of these layers in one day, but, as I've said, we probably can't.

There are many training theories, and they will all work to a greater or lesser extent, but this three-pronged attack of long, tempo and speed/strength has given me and my athletes the best return over the years.

One final point: Brendan Foster said that it was all very well doing all this training, you still had to screw yourself up on race day. Yes, some people say, train hard, race easy. Rubbish! Race easy if you're happy with that lukewarm, half-hearted, lacklustre personal best. But if you really want to know what you're made of, you've got to lay it all out there.

But how do you go about it?

CHAPTER 6

EASY – How can I make this easier?

"I had to change in the back seat of the car, jump out and run."

NOTHING CAN REPLACE hard work, but certain 'tricks' can give you the best chance of getting done what needs to be done. In this chapter, we'll focus on the vital habits of warming up and keeping a training log.

"We were stuck in traffic. I had to change in the back seat of the car, jump out and run."

"My warm-up was not good, I got tripped at the start, and I just felt flat."

"I knew I was going to beat the record from halfway through my warm-up."

When you need to do a hard session or when you get to a race – assuming you get there before our first witness (above) – probably the last thing you feel like doing is warming up. But experience – and science – has shown us that a decent warm-up can play a vital part in optimising your performance.

But what do you do? How much should you do? How long before the race should you do it? And how does it vary for different events?

Much of this is common sense.

One of my athletes thought that warming up consisted of sitting in the car with the heater on. Not so!

The wonderful machine that is your human body can do amazing things – given the right training **and** the right priming on the day.

It is unreasonable to ask your muscles to go from 'zero' (perhaps sat squashed in a car for an hour) to 'hero' race pace without warning.

In general, the shorter the race, the longer the warm-up. So, whilst sprinters will spend an hour or more jogging, stretching, striding, bouncing and sprinting (and 'shooting the breeze' and trash-talking), marathon runners need do very little.

However, for our classic distance events – 5km, 10km, half marathon – you should definitely warm up. It need take no more than 10–20 minutes, and you should complete it, if possible, about 10 minutes before the start time. And, obviously, at least in winter, you will keep more layers on in the warm-up than you will eventually race in.

The traditional warm-up is to jog until you break sweat, to stretch all the relevant muscles, and then to perform 4–6 stride-outs. These are acceleration runs of perhaps 60–100m, gradually reaching your race pace or a little faster.

You are simply ensuring that the start of the race is not a nasty shock to your muscles and cardiovascular system.

The other thing you are doing, of course, is warming up your mind. You are getting your brain used to the idea that you are about to **make an effort**.

As I've said, warming up is probably the last thing you feel like doing. Don't let your mind, desperate not to race, distract you ("Look, there's Ben, I'll go and have a chat," "Oooh, that coffee smells good"), but start your jog and you will come around.

Now, modern research has found that stretching has little benefit in the warm-up. I too would emphasise the jogging and the strides. I recommend jogging and then striding gently, doing any stretches that you want to, and then going back and doing a few faster strides.

Fitter runners can warm up for longer – a more extensive routine is not in any danger of exhausting them, as it might a less seasoned competitor.

Elite sportspeople develop their own idiosyncratic warm-up needs.

Jonah Barrington, the world champion squash player, had a warm-up that was so demanding that he eventually needed a warm-up for his warm-up!

Lee Calhoun, the double Olympic 110m hurdles champion, had a warm-up with 20 elements to it, starting with a half-mile jog, and including hops, sit-ups, side-bends, multiple dynamic stretches, bicycle kicks and even Cossack dance moves, and ending with 17 separate runs over 5–10 hurdles!

Conversely, Kenyan distance runners simply start even their hardest runs at a ridiculously easy pace (nine, 10, even 12-minute miles) and gradually build into the session.

Then again, I once watched Valeriy Borzov, the 100m and 200m champ from the 1972 Munich Olympic Games, towards the end of his career, warming up at Crystal Palace by trying to throw the hammer. Probably not recommended!

Geoff Capes, the 1974 Commonwealth champion shot-putter and later World's Strongest Man, got so hyped from his warm-up at the European Championships in Prague in 1978, that he manhandled ('Will Smithed') officials who said he was not wearing the right number – and he was promptly disqualified. Probably not recommended, either!

In the good old days of London buses all coming along at once, I was so late for a race on the other side of the city, that I had to change on the top deck of the 159 (much to the discomfiture of the old lady sitting next to me – I'm joking!), jump off, run to the start, and try and catch the field. At least my adrenalin was flowing!

Rod Dixon, the Kiwi Olympic bronze medallist, had his kit stolen before his 5,000m final at the 1978 Commonwealth Games. After rushing around trying to find it, failing and then attempting to borrow some, he had used up all his mental and emotional energy by the time the race started, so he consequently made no impact in the competition itself.

A student runner of my acquaintance once 'warmed up' for the Bath Half Marathon (start time: 11am) by mistakenly turning off all his alarms the night before, waking at 10:32am, running two miles to the start whilst eating a jacket potato and drinking a bottle of Lucozade, and having his Mum pin his number on for him in the pen at the back of the field.

He still overtook his Dad at 11 miles!

Which reminds me of Brian Green, UK 100m champion in the early 1970s. Arriving very late at a meeting, and hearing his event called, Green vaulted the fence, found his lane, got to his marks, the gun went and he won – dressed in his business suit!

And Henry Rono – four world records and two Commonwealth golds in 1978 – misread the time of his race and was still eating his burger and chips when it was called. Unflustered, he walked to the line, won the race, but missed the world record by two seconds!

Such shoddy timekeeping is again not recommended.

In the 1972 Munich Olympic Games, US sprint coaches misread the European 24-hour clock system for their charges' heat start time (reading 16:00 as 6pm), only saw that the races were lining up on TV, rushed to the stadium, but two out of the three – Eddie Hart and Rey Robinson (both world record holders) – were too late.

There are also tales of runners trying to psych each other out on the warm-up. If you think you've got a chance of winning the race and your main rival ambles through their warm-up and you charge through yours, perhaps you may go into the race with some confidence. Or, more importantly, maybe they won't!

The sheer muscularity of Peter Snell (800m and 1500m Olympic champion in 1964) would put his competitors off. YouTube 'Snell Modesto' for the best illustration of his power.

Of course, even in their warm-up, elite athletes can still amaze us. I remember watching the Soviet high jumper, Jüri Tarmak, prepare for the final at the Munich Games, where he eventually won gold. The warm-up bar was set at 2m, and he hopped over it!

For sheer dynamism, watch top sprinters leap in the air behind their blocks.

Warming down is another matter.

All elite runners will warm down after every hard session and every race. Keeping moving promotes blood circulation, which will start the process of clearing the muscles of lactic acid, thereby accelerating recovery (you can run again sooner, you lucky thing!) and avoiding stiffness.

Most runners will just jog for a few minutes to accomplish this.

Jack Buckner, the 1986 European 5,000m champion and, incidentally, the new UK Athletics CEO, said he relished **not** warming down after the last race of each season, knowing he had more than enough time to recover before his next test the following year.

Back to you and me.

If you want to put in a good performance, do warm up – at least jog and stride until you feel your body and your mind are ready.

Whatever your standard, and whatever your ambition, a good warm-up will help you – physically, mentally and emotionally – to achieve it.

And once you've done it, log it!

MONDAY. Ran three miles at 7am, then tried a few hill sprints, but gave up. Jogged back. Raining. Knackered. Call it four miles in total. Fed up.
TUESDAY. Rest.
WEDNESDAY. Left it till 9pm, ran five miles very slowly but felt OK.
THURSDAY. Gym – just arms, core and sit-ups.
FRIDAY. Jogged a mile, did sprints, then 4 x 2 minutes hard (two-minutes jog) – felt good, got further than before.
SATURDAY. Tail-walked at parkrun, then gym – just arms, core, sit-ups again.
SUNDAY. Ran 10 miles with Ben – felt strong and pushed for the last two.

Right from the start of your running journey, it's a good idea to keep a log of what you do.

You can do this in all sorts of ways now – from a simple piece of paper, through a physical diary or a spreadsheet on your laptop, to any number of online tracking systems.

And you can keep as much or as little information as you want. Some people will just write a couple of words about each session; others will write 'War and Peace', but the sort of notes I have made above are a good guide.

I think the trick is to write enough so you can look back and get an idea of how that day or week went, almost at a glance, without missing vital data (like the number of miles you did), but also without swamping the essential stuff in too much narrative!

How does this help you?

We all know that motivation can be a problem for runners, especially when you are starting out, but if you can look back at your log and see that you've completed, say, six weeks of running at least three times each week, then you are more likely to get out there this time.

It's a case of, "I've come so far; I don't want it all to mean nothing by giving up now."

Your log also gives you the means by which to compare your past and present. Have I improved? Well, two months ago, you ran that loop in 32 minutes and almost died (you noted, "Completely exhausted, sat on sofa and did not even shower for two hours") and today you did it in 27 minutes and felt great.

Or perhaps you tried a session of six lots of 60 seconds fast and 60 seconds jogging, but you had to walk between the last three efforts. Now you can do eight lots without stopping.

Your log also reminds you that you're doing OK, that you've put in a lot of work. Even when you may be in a bit of a slump – it all feels too much like hard work – you can look back and know you've been here before, that you have worked hard, and that it will come right.

I started my running log on 8th July 1973. Being a dinosaur, I have always used a manual diary to track my progress – and latterly my decline! But it means I can look back and relish some great sessions.

On 19th March 1985, for example, I can see that I jogged to Battersea Park track in London from where I worked at the time, warmed up and did 8 x 400m in an average of 68 seconds, with a strict 200m jog between. Sebastian Coe and his coach/father, Peter, were on the track that day. Very focused, I had to refuse Seb's request for my autograph!

I'd done that session many times before, and it was the first time that all of my efforts were under 70 seconds. (I was tempted to try and make it 10, all under 70, but sensed I would probably fail, and that the confidence boost from the 8 x 400m under 70 would be compromised if it became 10 x 400m under 72 seconds.)

That session gave me great self-belief – and the following Sunday I set my still-standing half marathon personal best.

By contrast, on 18th February 2020, I went to Basingstoke's Down Grange track, warmed up and slogged through the wind for 12-and-a-half laps to run 5km in 31:43; I then did 3 x 100m sprints and warmed down.

These sessions are worlds apart in terms of quality, but not in terms of commitment. I know that, in years to come, I will read about the latter with as much pride as I read about the former.

All of us runners – indeed everybody who strives to do anything that takes practice, patience and persistence – are on a journey. Every session is a part of the workout before it and the one after it – both in the sense that you feel Sunday's long run in your legs when you try to run fast on

Tuesday, **and** in the sense that all of your previous work has got you to where you are, to your new level, to the point where you are ready to cope with 30 miles a week, or with a 10km, or with running all the way up that hill.

We do it because we believe that all of that effort – let's be honest, all of that pain – must mean something. We can't have suffered for nothing. All of those sessions must weave together to constitute a whole that is more than the sum of their parts.

Keeping a training log helps us to see our trajectory, to plot our next tranche, and to identify our ultimate target – the target that has meaning for us.

Of course, along the way, a training log also helps get us out there to chase down that meaningful target.

A log will jog more than your memory.

CHAPTER 7

HARD – WHAT DO I NEED TO DO TO SUCCEED?

"The other 20%, Steve, are nutters!"

Geraint Thomas, Tour de France winner 2018

THE MOTHER OF *a young Olympic-hopeful swimmer once recounted their morning routine when her daughter was a young teenager: "Her alarm goes off and she comes and gets me up, and she goes back to bed. I go downstairs and make breakfast while she has another 15 minutes' sleep.*

*Then I get her up, she eats, and I take her to the pool. Why do we do it like this? Because it has to be **her** decision to do it."*

This is very telling, I think. Even at such a young age, the drive had to come from within the athlete. Her parents wisely did not impose their own ambitions on her, but if she wanted to do it, she would get up and start the day.

Beyond warming up, getting out and doing it, and then logging it, what else do we need to do?

We need to be quite hard on ourselves from time to time.

I have a very early breakfast meeting once a week, and a while ago I challenged myself to get up earlier than was strictly required to get there on time – and to go for a run. This meant getting up at about 4am. So, the night before, I would set the alarm, I would put my contact lenses out, I would set out my clothes, even, in these days of technical hosiery, putting my left sock to the left and my right sock to the right.

Why?

What are you on about, Steve?

What possible use is it arranging your socks like that?

Well, you see, I was minimising the obstacles to my getting up and getting out there, taking away all the possible barriers in my morning routine. We've all experienced those times when our determination to do something is hanging by a thread – and then some external hindrance comes along, such as the inability to find the right shoes – and we give up. Here, I could just swing out of bed and put on my socks automatically, almost in my sleep.

And, of course, pushing our limits in this way can lead us to do some 'nutty' things.

Some time ago, I visited a top physio, who had worked with hundreds of athletes of all standards. We naturally got chatting about the clients he'd had – anonymously, of course.

How would he categorise them?

"Fifty percent of the people who come in here, Steve, are serious athletes who want to adopt an aggressive approach to injury rehabilitation."

"Yes."

"Thirty percent would get better on their own."

"Yes, and the other 20%?" I asked.

"The other 20%, Steve, are nutters."

Emil Zátopek was a nutter. It's not just that he won four Olympic gold medals and is still the only man ever to win the 5,000m, 10,000m and marathon in a single Games (Helsinki 1952). It's more the training that got him there – the track sessions of 60 × 400m for days on end, running with his wife on his back, running in place on the laundry in the bath when his wife insisted that he help a bit more with household chores, holding his breath while on sentry duty during national service – and holding it till he blacked out. (How much discipline does **that** take?!) He was once described as being in body more machine than man, whilst remaining in spirit more boy than man. I think that's about right.

David Bedford certainly did nutty things. On 7th February 1970, while still a junior, the man who would set a world 10,000m record three years later, won the (separate) Southern Senior **and** Junior Cross-Country Championships on the same afternoon. He had about 20 minutes' rest between races, winning the senior event by 55 seconds and the junior event by 61 seconds. The idea to attempt something like that would only occur to a certain kind of person.

Similar was Steve Jones, marathon world record holder in 1984, who once won two 10km races on the same day.

Geraint Thomas, winner of the Tour de France in 2018, talked about training rides where he doesn't eat any carbs before going out on his bike for three hours: "You are grumpy because you are so hungry, but it trains the body in a particular way.

"But sometimes I like to test myself. Instead of going three hours, I will go four. Or five. Sometimes I go six hours. I am not even sure if that is good for you. But it is about proving something to myself."[12]

This is telling, isn't it? Whilst he's not at all sure a fasted session like that is physically good for him, he's damn sure it gives him a psychological edge.

Don Ritchie was not a nutter, but he was the greatest ultra-distance runner of all time. Among many, many great races, in 1978, he ran 100km on a track in 6:10:20. It is a world record that has never, at the time of writing, been beaten, and it equates to just faster than six-minute miles all the way!

But what fascinated me was his build-up to the race, which took place on a Saturday. Until Wednesday, he was still running 14 miles to work and 14 miles home at night. On the Thursday, he just ran to work, and on Friday, he rested.

I had the privilege of sharing road and track with Don many times, and I got to know him a little. I once asked this modest man why he ran so much so close to such an important race. "I may have benefitted from a

---

12 Newspaper cutting from *The Times*, 2018.

different tapering strategy, but three days seemed to be appropriate for me then."[13]

For anybody else, that would be nutty, but for a man who was used to churning out 28 miles day in, day out, 14 was an absolute holiday. Don't try this at home.

By now, you probably think I'm a nutter. Am I? I can only look back in agony.

When I was training for the Quadrathon (two-mile sea swim, 50km race walk, 100-mile cycle, marathon), my typical training day would consist of a run of up to 20 miles from home (Croydon) to work (central London). At lunchtime, I would race walk a few miles to the local pool, swim a mile, and walk back. Then at night I would cycle home via a circuitous route that occasionally included Brands Hatch, where most of the cycle leg would be taking place.

Needless to say, these lifestyle choices involved some careful logistical planning, which only occasionally went wrong, necessitating the re-wearing of yesterday's shirt, the borrowing of somebody else's towel, or wearing running shorts under my suit trousers.

The Quadrathon probably boasted the largest-ever collection of 'nutters' brought together in one place. It included the Crane brothers, Richard and Adrian, who had just run from one end of the Himalayas to the other, various world record holders at obscurely long distances, Boy George's brother, the bloke who held the Guinness World Record for carrying a hundredweight of coal on his back for an entire marathon, and who, when asked if he was all set for the bike leg, replied, "Yeah," patting his pockets, "got me fags…yeah, got me lighter," – and me.

Of course I'm a nutter!

---

13 Letter from Don to me.

Here are some more examples – and food for thought.

Back in the 1950s, 'Orrible' Horace Ashenfelter from Pennsylvania was an FBI agent and US 3,000m steeplechase champion. There were no full-time, professional athletes then, so he had to train for his event at odd hours of the day and night. This included running up and down the stairs in his office block during quiet periods, and hurdling benches in his local park late at night, for half an hour at a time. (He was sometimes stopped by the police.) He reckoned that anything that was hard was good training for an event as merciless as the steeplechase, and he won Olympic gold in 1952.

David Hemery was urged by his coach to turn up for pre-season training in a reasonably fit state. Hemery devised a routine of 50 press-ups, then 50 sit-ups, and finally an 800m stride-out…which he eventually repeated 20 times, for a 1,000 press-up, 1,000 sit-up, 10-mile run session! And this was **pre**- pre-season training, remember. His actual pre-season training as we have seen, included up to 23 miles of running a day – a long way for someone whose event lasted less than 50 seconds. "For me, the hardest way is the best way," he said.

The history of running is, of course, littered with athletes being hard on themselves. Jim Ryun, the American who ran a sub-four-minute mile in high school, frequently ran 40 × 400m – and performed weight-training in the intervals between the efforts!

Daley Thompson, in a recent interview, commented that today's athletes weren't as hard as those of his generation. He gave the example of Dave Ottley, an Olympic silver medallist in the javelin, who trained under Thompson's coach for a period in the 1980s, and who once complained about his sore stomach muscles. His coach asked why his stomach was sore, and Ottley said it was "all those sit-ups" that the coach was making him do. The coach had written, 'do 4–6 × 20 sit-ups (daily)'. Ottley had misread it as, do 46 × 20 sit-ups!

Thompson said that the point was that he did them without question.

And talking of athletes being obedient to their coaches…

A few years ago, I was advising Lisa, a runner who wanted to mark her 50th birthday by running 50 miles over one weekend. We devised a training programme and a route, and she set to. Injuries and other commitments intervened to make it a less than perfect build-up, and two weeks before the scheduled ultra-run, she emailed me to say that she had lost so much training (and confidence) that she was going to do 50km instead.

I thought about it and then replied along the lines of: "You can do 50km if you like but you will regret it afterwards. This is not about it being manageable or easy to do, or anything like that. It is because it is difficult to do, that you are doing it, and why we run marathons and test ourselves. I repeat, it is precisely because it is difficult that you are doing it, and why you wanted to run 50 miles in the first place."

And then the clincher: "And, anyway, I will shout at you if you don't do it." (I know my athletes!)

The lady in question said that, once she had received that email, she simply decided she could do it – and did it.

What does all of this mean for you?

Well, as I have said, go gently at first, build up gradually, let your body recover between sessions, schedule easy runs…but, once in a while, really go for it!

Sprint at the end of a run, do that extra hill, run an extra mile, do speedwork. It won't be easy, but it sure is satisfying afterwards! And, let's face it, as a percentage of that week's overall training time, you're only in what I call 'the pain box' for a comparatively short period.

As one experienced fell runner said to a newbie, "Anyone can be fit. It's being hard, that's hard."

CHAPTER 8

ASK – WHY AM I DOING THIS SPECIFIC SESSION?

"No, no, no. You're missing the whole point!"

The GB 24-hour squad for the 1996 European Championships, with the author middle back

AT A GB Ultra-distance squad weekend in 1995, one international 100km runner said that every Tuesday night, he ran 8 x 600m hills as hard as he could.

"Hmm," the national coach opined. "I'd rather see you preface that with a hard 15-miler. It'd be better for your endurance."

There was silence, and some murmurs of agreement. Then I spoke up.

"Why? That is the one session in his week when he works to keep his fastest gears in order. You're missing the whole point of the session."

(Yes, even as would-be 24-hour internationals, we were instructed to keep the speedwork going. The theory is that all your gears are connected. If you're faster at a mile, you'll be faster at 10km, assuming you do the longer endurance work too; if you're faster at 10km, you'll be faster at the marathon; and a faster marathon runner will always beat a slower one at 100km and 24 hours, if their endurance training is similar.)

But the main point here is – always know why you are doing a session.

In the early days, of course, you just run. You do this run today, so that, in a few weeks' time, you will be able to run further or faster or easier.

But, as time goes on, we can add a bit more science.

In terms of a typical jogger/runner, we would encourage them to run a bit further, on some days to run a bit faster, and to build into their weekly programme a clear pattern of hard and easy runs.

'Run a bit faster' then can take on many forms, and here we can bump up against lots of lovely, confusing words like intervals, repetitions, speedwork, tempo, time trials, hills and fartlek.

Fartlek, Steve?

Stop sniggering at the back. It's a Swedish word meaning 'speed play'.

For the purposes of this chapter, I won't go into all of these.

The point I am making is that one should always know why one is doing any given run, workout or session.

And it brings us back to having a target.

In simple terms, if you've got a 10km race in a few weeks, you are more likely to go out on a wet Tuesday night and run that five miles you have scheduled. If you have a mile race coming up, you are more likely to do that 6 x 60 seconds hard, 60 seconds jog, session. If you are doing a half marathon in eight weeks' time, you know that your long run of six miles is insufficient preparation, so you make plans to run further each Sunday between now and then.

Looking at it from the other end of the equation, the mistake that runners make the most is doing a moderately long, moderately hard run most of the time – and wondering why they're not improving as fast as they would like.

Any running will, of course, eventually lead to improvement, but it's the 'outlier' sessions that will bring it the fastest.

The human body can only take so much, can only improve at a certain rate, so, yes, most of our runs will be easy to moderate, but it is your once-a-week long run and your once or twice-a-week speedier sessions that are going to maximise this.

Just as doing the same thing over and over again and expecting different results is one definition of insanity, running the same speed for the same distance over and over again and expecting massive improvement is also a bit bonkers.

Running is not hugely technical, is it? When one of my friends heard I was writing a book basically about how to run, they asked, "What? Is it just going to be 200 pages of 'left, right, left, right'?"

Hilarious!

Most other sports contain a far higher level of skill than running demands. Just think of the hand-eye coordination involved in ball sports; even the technique involved in other endurance events such as swimming, cycling and rowing.

In that respect, you are lucky. There's not much to get right. Or get wrong. But you still have to undertake the right mix of work, plus all of the nutrition, hydration and recovery habits that optimise your ability to do the best training.

Here are two examples of fairly non-technical, but still well thought-out, training routines from the world of cycling:

American Greg LeMond won the Tour de France three times (1986, 1989 and 1990). In the winters, he lived in Minnesota, where the snow made cycling difficult, so every morning he would go down to his den, get on his stationary bike and, once warmed up, pedal furiously in the highest gear for rep after rep. The observer noted that no attention was paid to form – to pedalling in neat cycles, to limiting upper body movement and such. It was all about the effort. After this, he went cross-country skiing for several hours to build stamina. LeMond felt that most cyclists downplayed the intensity in winter, and this was one way to get ahead of them.

Chris Hoy's needs as a sprinter were very different from LeMond's as an endurance cyclist, but the intensity is common to both.

You may have seen the documentary about Hoy's training before the London 2012 Olympic Games. If so, you will have seen the crucifying squat sessions and stationary bike intervals that his coach put him through – rendering him unable to walk properly the next day. Then remember that moment in the keirin final when he was challenged on the last bend by the German rider, Maximilian Levy. You can almost see the Scottish rider calling on his quads for more power at that point. Hoy held Levy off and won his sixth Olympic gold – and had Steve Redgrave (only five Olympic golds!) congratulate him in person. **That** was why he did those sessions.

They were worth it for the 0.06 seconds he won by.

So, he certainly knew why he was doing them.

CHAPTER 9

CHANGE – WHEN SHOULD I SHAKE THINGS UP?

"You're doing too much."

The last desperate hours of a 24-hour track race

"YOU'RE NOT GIVING yourself a chance to do the quality. Look here, you're trying to do your fast work on a Tuesday, when you've done your very longest run on the Sunday, and then not recovered properly on the Monday – doing two 10-milers. You've got to add more 'hard and easy', more 'light and shade.'"

Paul ran twice every day but was not reaching his ultra-running goals. He asked for my help. A quick glance at his training log showed me that it was obvious he was making one of runners' most common mistakes.

When you've built up to a decent amount of mileage per week, you then have the opportunity to vary it – long runs, hard runs, easy runs, hill sessions, speed sessions. So, we runners go off and try to do that, but it's hard.

As I have said, what I find is that the runners will do all the sessions, but too many of them are a moderate-length run at a moderate pace. Like Paul, but in a different way, there is little or no variety. It's comparatively easy to go out and run steadily for a time; it's hard to put yourself through a real quality session.

And, to really improve, that's what you have to do.

Crucially, it means running very easily – or not at all – on the days when you are not going hard or long. (That's what Paul wasn't doing – he was so keen to improve that he ran too hard every day. He never got the chance to recover and put in the real quality when it mattered.)

I would advocate doing a really hard session and then jogging very easily until you are recovered. That may mean for one day, though it's probably more likely to be for two or even three days.

Benji Durden ran a 2:09:57 marathon in Boston in 1983 by running some incredibly hard sessions – a long warm-up, what he called 'a track monster' of five lots of 2,000m fast (400m jog), 1,000m fast (400m jog) and then a fast 'warm-down' over some serious hills – but then just jogging for 30–45 minutes for the next few days.

What should your quality session look like?

Long runs are easy to explain: you run a bit further than you have up to now, at a pace that is easy to start with, and it only gets really tough in the last quarter of the run.

For speed sessions, I would highly recommend repetitions. What do I mean? First, you need to warm up well – jog for at least a mile, walk for a minute, and then do some strides – accelerations for 50–60 yards, gradually building up to top speed. Stretch if you want to, but in any case give yourself a moment to recover.

Then – the hard work – run fast for 30 seconds, jog for 30 seconds, and repeat this five times. You will need to start at a pace that lets you complete the set of five without walking, and so that your last fast effort is as fast as your first – if not faster.

Build this up to eight repetitions (reps) over a few weeks, and then switch to 60-second efforts with 60-second jogs. Start with four efforts and four jogs. It is critical that you keep the jog going between the efforts – do not walk. The value of this session is in its continuous demands – and the fact that you do not recover fully between efforts.

These 60-second efforts will naturally feel a lot longer than the 30-second ones. Because they are, Steve, because they are!

Do the same thing with these, adding one or two efforts each week until you have done 10 in one go.

Now – the difficult bit – change the jog to a 'float'. What do I mean? Instead of jogging at a snail's pace between the efforts, hit a speed between that and your steady run pace.

This makes the session a lot harder because you are recovering even less between the efforts.

But do them right, and these sessions are gold dust.

You are training your muscles to cope with fatigue, you are running just over and under your race pace and, if you keep these up for about six weeks, you will find that you will possess another gear in races from a mile to a marathon.

The ultimate kind of these sessions is 6 x 2 minutes effort / 2 minutes float. I have experimented with these sessions a lot over the years. I find that less than two-minute efforts produce less of a training effect, and doing longer efforts tend to make the quality suffer, and you are not working on your race pace quite so effectively. So, two-minute efforts it is! At least, for me.

Again, four of these is good, but eight of these I found too much. So, six seems to be golden.

The speed will vary according to your strengths and goals, but I found that my hard pace was about mile PB speed, and my float pace was long run pace. Let me emphasise – definitely **not** a jog!

There you go! For the established, ambitious runners amongst you, vary your runs to make sure you recover properly between the key sessions. Put the long runs in, do repetitions, building gradually, if you like, to the magic 6 x 2 minutes effort / 2 minutes float. And, of course, work towards a target to motivate you when it gets tough.

As for Paul?

He followed my advice and was national 100km champion in a shiny new personal best six months later!

CHAPTER 10
STAY – WHY SHOULD I KEEP THINGS THE SAME?

"I basically train the same way every week of the year."

Rob de Castella, middle with moustache

MONDAY. Ran 10km in the morning, gym session at noon, and ran 16km at night.

TUESDAY. Ran 10km, gym session, and ran 10km plus sprints.

WEDNESDAY. Ran 10km, gym session, and ran 29km.

THURSDAY. Ran 10km, gym session, and ran 8 x 400m.

FRIDAY. Ran 10km, gym session, and ran 18km.

SATURDAY. Ran 20km plus hill sprints and then 10km.

SUNDAY. Ran 35km and then 8km.

SO SAID ROB de Castella – the above routine was what he followed every week – and it worked.[14] (Sometimes it did vary slightly. I attended a Q&A session with the man in the early 1980s, and he admitted that occasionally he was so tired, that he only did 8km in the mornings, instead of 10. There were murmurs around the room that he was human after all.)

Once he reached world-class level in 1980 (10th in the Moscow Olympic marathon), the Australian set his sights on five more major marathons. Fukuoka in Japan was regarded as the highest-class race in the world. This was an era before the big city marathons like London and New York City exerted their dominance.

Fukuoka was his target in 1981 and he won in a world-record time of 2:08:18. Alberto Salazar had run 2:08:13 in New York City earlier that year, but the course was later found to be slightly short.

'Deek', as de Castella is known, then won Commonwealth Gold in Brisbane 1982, in a mammoth tussle with Juma Ikangaa of Tanzania, with the lead changing hands several times in the final miles. (Mike Gratton gives us an eye-witness account of this race in his Foreword to this book.)

The year 1983 started with a showdown in Rotterdam between the two greatest marathoners in the world – Deek and Salazar, who had won New York City three times (1980–1982) and Boston once. Other dangerous competitors were Rodolfo Gómez of Mexico (second to Salazar in New York City) and Carlos Lopes of Portugal (1976 Olympic 10,000m silver medallist), running his second marathon, having failed to finish his first after bumping into a spectator in New York City in 1982.

It came down to Deek and Lopes, with the Australian prevailing by two seconds in a very fast 2:08:37. This surprised many commentators as

---

14 *Deek*, Rob de Castella with Mike Jenkinson, pages 33–34.

Deek's raw speed was nowhere near the Portuguese man's – 28:12.2 for 10km against Carlos' eventual 27:17:48.

Deek then won the inaugural World Championships marathon in Helsinki later that year.

These four triumphs meant he only had the biggest prize left to win, to complete his CV.

But in the Los Angeles Olympic marathon in 1984, he was well beaten, as were the entire field by a now more-experienced Lopes, who ran away from John Treacy of Ireland (silver medal) and Charlie Spedding of Great Britain (bronze) to win in 2:09:21. Deek was fifth in 2:11:09.

My point is this: Rob de Castella got great results for many years by training basically the same way every week of the year. And let's face it, that weekly routine covered all the bases – endurance, speed-endurance, sheer speed, leg strength via hills and so on. But perhaps he should have changed it up at some point, because it was obvious that, in Los Angeles, he came up against a runner who had by now learnt how to run the marathon, and crucially had significantly better basic (10km) speed.

If it ain't broke, fix it!

CHAPTER 11

PROGRESS – WAS IT BETTER THAN YESTERDAY?

"Progress, not perfection." – Robert McCall, The Equalizer

SHE STOOD BY the side of the track after the last 400m effort, and she looked really fed up.

"What's wrong, Lorna? That was a good session."

"Yeah, I guess," she said. "I think I'm improving. I know I <u>ought</u> to be improving. But how do I know if I really am?"

It's a very good question. Every ambitious runner naturally would like some indication that all the hard work is paying off, but you don't want to be running time trials every day, or all-out races every week.

Now, we all know that there are apps that can bombard us with all the data that we need. Or do they? Or do we? How many times have you felt aggrieved that, when you've pushed really hard, your phone labels your run 'unproductive' or merely 'maintaining'?

Let's get real – not virtual.

The simplest 'real' way to find out if you've progressed is to run a favourite route as fast as you can, and see if you can achieve your best-ever time.

That, of course, is hard. And how do you know if it was just because you tried that bit harder this time? It might just be that you've improved your willpower, rather than your fitness. But, hang on, that is also something to be valued: runners need to develop their mental strength (willpower) just as surely as they need to condition their muscles.

But it would be nice to have something rather more objective. So, why not run your favourite route at the same speed as before, but see if your heart rate is lower? That is a great indication of increased fitness.

As is the time it takes you to recover. How long does it take your heart rate to come down to 80, say (about the normal resting rate in an untrained person)? How much more quickly does that happen than before?

Or let's take a typical interval session, like the one that Lorna was doing.

Let's say you run a session of 6 x 400m with a 200m walk in between. And let's say you can average 1:45 for those six efforts.

How many ways can you change that session to make it harder?

By my reckoning, there are at least four major variables.

One: you can run more efforts – so eight or 10, instead of six. Two: you can run them faster – try and average 1:40, then 1:35, and so on. Three: you can take less rest – jog the 200m recovery, or even cut it to 100m. Four: you can run longer efforts – if you can run 600m at the same speed as you did for the 400m – keeping all other variables the same – then that is definite progress.

But be careful here, because it is very difficult to go from 400m to 600m (a 50% jump, remember) whilst keeping the same recovery, and I would argue that, since you had a recovery jog of half the distance for the 400m, you should also have that for the 600m.

So, the 'equivalent' step-up session from 6 x 400m with a 200m jog, is 6 x 600m with a 300m jog. The progression resides in the fact that you are maintaining the same speed for 50% longer – with the other variables unchanged – half of the effort's distance for the jog. An average of 1:45 for 400m becomes 2:37.5 for 600m.

There's no getting away from the truth in those numbers. But there are also more subjective measures that I value highly.

If you run a certain distance in a certain time, or complete a particular interval (effort) session, **and you feel better than you ever did before** doing it, then you have made progress.

If you finish a punishing hill session, say, and you still feel fresh, then that is improvement.

If you find that, for the first time, you can sprint at the end of a particular distance run, or maintain your speed to the top of that long hill, then your speed – and strength – are heading in the right direction.

(Remember: the ability to sprint at the end of a run or a race is not just down to your speed. You also have to possess the stamina and speed-endurance to be able to preserve that bit of speed through the preceding miles and still have it to deploy at the finish.)

Runners use key sessions to test themselves before big races. They normally only do this when they are pretty sure that they are fitter than ever, in order to be certain of receiving that vital confidence boost. But the sessions have to be relevant to the target race.

I have talked about Brendan Foster winning the 1974 European 5,000m by injecting a 59-second lap with five to go. His crucial session in preparing for this was that series of very fast 200m efforts, with only 30 seconds between. Completing these sessions taught him that he could indeed kick in the middle of a race and not get into debilitating oxygen debt.

Mara Yamauchi, the third fastest British female marathon runner of all time, undertook a session that emphasised the sustained speed that event demands. At altitude in Arizona, she completed a session of 3 x 5km on the track with a one-lap jog recovery. She achieved times of 17:18, 17:23 and 17:28.

Before a major ultra-distance race, I used a sequence of three sessions, a few days apart, to test myself.

The first was a 35-mile trail run: here, it was more important for me to finish it feeling relatively fresh, than to run my fastest-ever time. In my race, I would be going 62 or more miles, remember. The second was a hilly 10-miler, where I did try to set a new personal best. And the third was a track session – a continuous series of 400m, 600m and 800m, with little recovery.

I rather liked this last session to have a double target – running the efforts at fast speeds but also achieving an overall PB for the session. Because of this idea, I would make my workout a sequence of 400m, 600m, 400m, 800m, 400m, 800m, 400m, 600m, 400m, with 200m jogs between each (but not after the last 400m!). If you care to add this up, the total distance is 6,400m, or basically four miles. As I say, I enjoyed the challenge of running it all fast – without compromising the speeds of the reps.

Completing those three sessions in better shape than ever before gave me the confidence to attack the upcoming ultra-distance race.

And Lorna? Well, we looked back at her training diaries and identified several key markers from six months before. Over the next few weeks, she undertook four trials to test her raw speed, her short-distance speed-endurance, her longer-interval tolerance, and finally her stamina. Two of these were all-out efforts; and the other two were judged on heart rate.

In all four dimensions, she was streets ahead of where she had been half a year before.

She was finally delighted, rather than fed up, and begged to be allowed to repeat the tests every three months. I said do them annually, and we compromised on every six months!

CHAPTER 12

RUT – HOW DO I GET OUT OF THIS RUT?

"Run from zombies if you have to, but run."

"NOT THIS HILL again!"

"I'm so bored with this route."

"During Covid-19, when we couldn't go out, I was desperate to. Now I can't be bothered."

During the Covid-19 pandemic, lots of people took up running. Well, with gyms closed and most organised sport simply not happening, it was one of the few things you were allowed to do to be active and keep fit.

But the restrictions meant that we found ourselves with limited running options. We were told, for instance, not to venture far from home, not to drive to exercise further afield, and not to meet others to do so.

We don't have those restrictions anymore, thank goodness, but sometimes we all get stuck in a running rut – locked in lockdown lockstep, if you will.

So here are a few ideas on how to mix things up:

A TO B. If your running route is boring, try going A to B. Get a bus or a train, or some kind soul, to drop you a few miles from home, and run back – it's far easier and more motivating to run in one direction than do a loop. It seems 'right' in the same way that it seemed right to our ancestors to migrate along the primeval pathways.

BUDDY UP. Now that we can exercise with others, find a friend, colleague or online contact whose pace, personality and patter are congenial enough for you to run alongside for half an hour or so. You're far more likely to keep that date with your running schedule, if you're also keeping it with a fellow runner.

CLUB NIGHT. At its most formal, running with others can mean finding and perhaps joining a club. There are likely to be many in your local area, most catering for all abilities, with a variety of organised sessions to motivate you and introduce you to like-minded souls. Have a look online.

DOG DAYS. If you have one, or have access to one, then running with a dog is great fun. Make sure they are fit enough to do the distance you have in mind and be sure to keep them under control – especially around livestock. You'll find they're far more intelligent and reliable than any human running companion!

THE RUN OF LIFE

EARLY DOORS. Many of you may run first thing in the morning, but for those of you who don't, try it! It can take a little getting used to (after all, your body is not quite as awake as it is later), but if you do venture out before it's light, you'll find a different world, one that's all your own. That time is your time: no one can take it away. And I promise you that you'll feel great all day!

FARTLEK. Yes, again, stop giggling on the back row. Fartlek is a Swedish word meaning 'speed play'. It came to prominence with the exploits of world-record-breaking Swedish milers, Gunder Hägg and Arne Andersson, in the 1940s, who would go out into the woods and perform unstructured speedwork – jog a mile, sprint to that tree, jog a bit, sprint up that hill, do a fast half-mile. It's having fun while working hard. It avoids the dread associated with a more formal interval session, where you know you've got five more of these blooming efforts to go.

GOALS. This is something I bang on about a lot. If your motivation is lacking, set yourself a goal – not too ambitious and not too distant, but a personal best, a running streak, a race or an accomplishment that you know is going to make it more likely you'll get out of that door to run.

HOLIDAY. If running is important to you, consider a running holiday. You'll get most benefit if you go with an organised group – with runs of various distances and speeds laid on for you every day, plus talks and discussions on aspects of running. You'll find you'll do a bit more than normal – and you'll come back motivated to keep the improvement going.

INTERVALS. If you feel that your running is stagnating, then intervals may be the answer. Unlike fartlek, intervals are structured speedwork, and they can be as simple as doing 6 x 30 seconds hard, 30 seconds jog – or 4 x all-out 60m hills (strict jog back down) – in the middle of a run. Most runners are guilty of too many easy to moderate miles – intervals break that cycle.

JUST JOG 10. If you really don't want to run, then I have a rule – just go out and jog for 10 minutes, and if you really don't want to do any more after that, fine, you can walk back home. But you'll almost always find yourself doing a decent run.

KIT YOURSELF OUT. Looking good is feeling good, so treat yourself to some new kit from time to time. The right kit will not only make running that little bit easier, but also lift your sartorial spirits.

LOOK OUT. I know some runners, who, when they lack motivation, set themselves a list of items to look out for on their runs (there are apps with suggestions). Examples include a deer, a celebrity, a body of water, a llama, money on the ground, even a good deed to be done.

MUSIC. If you always run with music, maybe unplug for a more mindful running experience. If you don't, consider tuning in for the motivation it provides – *Born to Run*, *When the Going Gets Tough*, *Something Inside So Strong* – I know, I know, I'm showing my age through my musical tastes!

NEW LOCATION. If running from A to B presents too many logistical problems, then simply get yourself to a new location and run there. Take the opportunity to run in the woods, along the beach, round a lake, or simply somewhere a little removed from your usual stomping, stamping ground.

OPPOSITE ATTRACTION. Simply run your regular routes in the opposite direction – you'll see things differently, you won't get intimidated by that hill at two miles, and you'll have a brand-new route without having to devise one. Warning: even though you are, by definition, in familiar territory, it is surprisingly easy to miss a turn when you are going the other way!

PLAN TO NAIL IT. Setting yourself a goal (above) implies giving yourself a plan. "If I'm going to do that 10km in eight weeks, then I better run more than three miles this Sunday."

QUOTE ME. Famous sayings about running, as well as from books, films, songs, videos and poetry can motivate you, because the will to win is nothing without the will to prepare, and if you can fill the unforgiving minute with sixty seconds' worth of distance run, baby, you were born to run!

RACE ACE. Again, I've said this before, but entering a race will really help your day-to-day running motivation.

STRAVA STRIVER. This app opens up a whole new way of recording your running performances and route segments, and sharing and comparing them with your peers, lending your running its own cheerleading support community.

TRACK HACK. There's no denying that a 400m running track is an intimidating environment, but there's also nothing like it for getting the best out of yourself. Have a go – warm up and set yourself a simple session to complete – something like, run 400m at a brisk pace, jog 200m, sprint 200m, walk 400m – and repeat. There's no hiding place, but there's also no comparison with the satisfaction you'll get from committing yourself to it.

U-TURN. Sometimes, when I know I should be trying to run hard and I just don't want to, I run as far as I can bear in one direction, trying to go fast. I note the time, turn round, and try and get back faster.

VESTED INTEREST. Wearing a vest – male or female cut – rather than a t-shirt can seem a little hardcore, especially in winter, but you'll be surprised how quickly you warm-up, and on how few days you need more covering. Your vest also proclaims that you're a runner – and you'll unconsciously run faster as a consequence.

WATCH OUT. If you run with a watch or Garmin®, consider ditching it on at least some runs – it is quite liberating. If you never run with one, how about wearing one and noting your splits to see how your pace varies across the run?

XANADU. Sometimes when you are running, you get – usually unexpectedly – in the zone, in flow, you hit nirvana, Xanadu, a purple patch, a zen-like state, where you feel you could run forever. It doesn't happen very often, I grant you, but when it does, relish it, hold on to it for as long as you can, log it and remember it.

'YOU TIME'. Sometimes, it's important to reconnect with why you run. Unless you're a pro like Mo, it's probably a personal thing, an experiment of one, a very individual journey – 'you time'.

ZOMBIES, RUN! This app takes your run to a new level of immersion, excitement and enjoyment, as you run and automatically collect supplies to help your town survive a zombie apocalypse!

CHAPTER 13

BALANCE – WHAT IS THE BEST THING FOR ME TO DO TODAY?

"You're leaving it all on the training track."

The author (right) competing in the London to Brighton Walk, 1983

BACK IN 1982, when I was still a race walker, I was in good form. I had finally that year got under 80 minutes for 10 miles and, with the National Championships in Sheffield coming up, even with the expected hilly course, I was looking for a big personal best.

Trouble was, I felt **too** good, and on my usual commute to work on the Friday, the day before the big race, I was flying and couldn't resist going for my best-ever time on the roughly seven-mile route I'd done hundreds of times before. And indeed, I took it down from 57 to 55 minutes.

The next day, unsurprisingly, I was knackered, struggled round and finished outside 80 minutes.

Of course, you can shoot yourself in the foot in other ways. One marathoner whom I was coaching felt so fresh on his taper week before London, that he decided to clear out the garage **and** the loft, leaving him aching and incredibly stiff in muscles he didn't normally use. Needless to say, the race was a disaster.

Even top international runners have been tackled by their teammates who see them wasting their race on the training track.

Of course, there is a fine line between doing the hard sessions that will lead to a peak performance and going over the top. It takes a very self-aware runner, or a very firm coach, to keep the athlete on the right side of that line.

And sometimes it's intuition. In 1974, Steve Ovett had already shown great potential (he had been European Junior 800m champion the year before) and the European Championships (senior) were coming up. But he was ill. Harry Wilson, his coach, nevertheless took him to a training camp at Merthyr Mawr in South Wales, which boasts the highest sand dunes in Europe.

Naturally, Ovett didn't feel like doing much, but Wilson persuaded him to run up The Big Dipper (you can imagine!) just once. The runner later recalled doing the effort and lying at the top, being ill, feeling terrible.

But the next day he felt better and was soon able to resume the training that would earn him an amazing silver medal in the European 800m.

Later in his career, Ovett would complete sessions like 2 x 600m, with each 600m broken down into 400m in 50 seconds (sometimes even 49 seconds, a sub-world-record pace for 800m), a 100m float and a 100m sprint!

Observers talk of his greatest-ever session being a 200m/400m/600m with just 30 seconds between each, with target times of 25, 50 and 75 seconds, each again under world-record pace for the 800m. Ovett pleaded with Wilson to be excused from the session, but in the end he completed it – though just failing to hit all the times, recording 25, 50 and 76 seconds!!

No wonder he never came to anything!

Obviously, you've got to build up to that sort of thing; you've not got to do it too often; and, as a coach, you've got to be sure it's not going to break the athlete.

For us mere mortals, especially if coming back from illness, injury or any other interruption to training, we just have to ask ourselves, "What is the best thing I can do today, to put myself in the best position to be able to carry on with my schedule sometime in the coming days?"

The answer may well be, "Nothing!"

And there is always hydration and nutrition to consider. There are also proactive recovery aids, such as stretching (warm muscles only), massage, foam-rolling and ice baths, alongside more active recovery through jogging (or cycling or swimming) and strides.

A note on hydration:

Science is now of the opinion that being over-hydrated is much more dangerous than being dehydrated. The reason is that over-hydration dilutes your mineral salts, your electrolytes, to a dangerous degree, risking even your life. Being dehydrated, of course, will also mean a degradation in performance, and can itself be life-threatening in extreme cases, but all athletes should certainly be aware of the hazards of going too far either way.

As well as the above techniques, as we've seen in our garage and loft-clearing marathoner, there is every other area of your life to monitor as well. You don't want to be on your feet for hours the day or two before a marathon – even at the expo! Don't spend hours in the kitchen. Cutting the grass can wait. DIY can wait. Playing football with the kids will have to be gently postponed.

It is figuratively as well as literally a marathon and not a sprint.

It takes discipline and courage to play the long game.

CHAPTER 14
STREAK – IS STREAKING GOOD FOR ME?

"He didn't say anything about not running on it."

Ron Hill, pictured after his record attempt at the 30,000m in October 1969, with crowds around him in the pouring rain

THE DISCIPLINE OF streaking.

On 31st January 2017, Ron Hill did not run. In the preceding months, we'd had the Brexit vote and its aftermath, Donald Trump's election and Leicester City winning the Premier League title, but Hill's inactivity was by far the biggest and most surprising news in my world.

You see, Ron Hill, European marathon champion in 1969 and Commonwealth marathon champion in 1970, had run every day from 20th December 1964 to 30th January 2017 – a world record. Actually, that's not strictly true – he'd also run twice a day (and once on Sundays) for the first 26.2 years of that streak.

Naturally, the need to keep this up saw him do some strange things – like running round an airport lounge, like 'running' on crutches after bunion surgery, like running more than twice a day when he crossed the international date line – just to make sure.

There was also the story that, after one knee operation, his doctor told him not to walk on it for at least two weeks. Hill naturally ran ("he didn't say anything about not running on it.").

Is that a good thing or a bad thing?

On 7th September 2013, I decided that, if I wanted to keep remotely fit, amongst other resolutions, I would have to go to the gym at least twice a week.

So far, I have managed to keep it up – just about. Lockdown, of course, complicated this – no amount of determination would open their doors to me during those periods, so I bought some weights and enforced a minimum weekly routine at home.

But earlier there had been another challenge – one that can show us a lot about the nature of streaking – and those who do it.

My partner's mother died in February 2018. We got the call that she was gravely ill early in the morning and dashed up to Norfolk to see her. Unfortunately, we were too late to see her alive.

We stayed in Norfolk and spent the rest of the week making the necessary arrangements.

But I had only gone to the gym once that week.

Problem. Big problem.

Then I had a brilliant idea!

We called in at the local leisure centre, said we were moving to the area, and asked to look round the gym. We signed the forms and, once in the gym, I wandered around, picked up one dumbbell and put it down again.

For the next three months, I was plagued with text messages inviting me to join the gym at their specially reduced rate that would only last until midnight that day!

But it was a small price to pay for getting in that second gym 'session'.

Now, you're absolutely right: what earthly value was there in picking up one dumbbell and putting it down again? Well, what possible benefit did Ron Hill gain from doing a mile on crutches?

Do we own the streak? Or does the streak own us?

Are we, as some streakers have it, simply too weak to stop?

The way I look at it is this: if I had not done that second 'session' that week, it would have been all too easy not to do one when things got difficult another week. A streak is like a deal with the devil: if I promise to keep you (the streak) going – to run every day whatever the circumstances, to go to the gym twice a week however inconvenient – then you (the streak) will provide me with the motivation to maintain it when enthusiasm, rather than opportunity or time, is what is lacking.

It's artificial, yes, but it offers mere mortals like me a framework to hang on to, a way to keep things going, a means by which to never give up.

Never give up! Derek Turnbull taught me that. Remember him? Twice I stayed on his farm near Invercargill on New Zealand's South Island, and I shared runs with the man who ran a 2:41 marathon at the age of 65, and who won gold medals at 800m, 1,500m, 5,000m, 10,000m, marathon and cross-country at the World Masters Games. When we were leaving, I asked him to autograph my training diary, and the only other thing he wrote apart from his name were the three words, "Never give up!"

Streaks are simply an extreme manifestation of never giving up – because they are binary. Either you ran today or you didn't, either you went to the gym twice this week or you failed. Streaks take the decision out of your hands. As Ron Hill said more than once, because of the streak, it was never a question of **whether** he would run, simply **when** and **where**.

But it's got to be the **right** streak.

A little while ago, I decided to start my days by performing 75 press-ups, then taking the dog for a walk or run, and then drinking apple cider vinegar (ACV) – supposedly great for kick-starting your metabolic rate in the mornings.

It got to be too much. I would lie in bed dreading the moment I would have to get up and do the press-ups, and then drink the wretched shudder-inducing ACV. It was self-defeating. I gave up the press-ups and the vinegar (the dog wouldn't let me give up the other bit).

I've got a few streaks going at the moment – the aforementioned gym visits, running at 5am before my networking breakfast each Thursday, covering a certain mileage each week, and running certain races every year. So far, they are good streaks, not bad streaks, but if they turn bad, I hope I'll have the strength to stop.

Though my friends doubt that.

CHAPTER 15

PERSIST – HOW CAN I OVERCOME THIS SETBACK?

"Two laps to go." "I'm sure I've only got one!"

THE 1993 NATIONAL 100km Championships were held round the three-mile lap of Holme Pierrepont Country Park at the National Water Sports Centre in Nottingham. It was my first 100km race; I thought I might be able to go under nine hours, and sure enough, that was fairly comfortably within my reach, as I came round knowing I had one lap to go.

"Two laps to go," an official shouted to me.

Not what you need.

Luckily, a runner I half-knew, who was supporting someone else, hearing my protest, immediately yelled: "Keep running, Steve, I'll sort it out." And he was able to get a message to me a couple of minutes later, confirming that I was indeed on my last lap.

That was a setback that could be swiftly overcome.

"My knee's still sore, I've had Covid-19 – I really don't think I'll be ready for London."

Probably the single question I get asked most by my athletes is this: "I've got this problem. Can I still do it?"

Well, a problem is a problem – unless it's a blessing in disguise!

David Bedford often put in 200 miles of running a week, but his finest race – his world record 10,000m at Crystal Palace in 1973 – came as the result of a slight injury that made him ease back in the lead-up to that event. It was the final piece of the jigsaw – one that made him fresh for the race, but one that he would not have agreed to, unless he was forced into it.

That's what I mean by a blessing in disguise.

There is a story that, the first time he did 200 miles in a week, he was sitting in the bath on the Sunday night, counting up his runs, when he realised that he'd only done 198 miles. He got out of the bath, went out and ran three miles, before getting back in the tub. When friends asked why he had done three miles instead of two, he said: "Well, you can't call two miles a run, can you?!"

On the other hand, Paula Radcliffe went into the Athens 2004 Olympic marathon as overwhelming favourite, having set an astonishing world record of 2:15:25 the year before – minutes faster than any other female has ever achieved. But she had sustained a leg injury shortly before the Games, and the anti-inflammatories she took hindered her stomach's food absorption. In effect, she started the marathon with no fuel inside her, ran incredibly bravely, but had to drop out at 23 miles (when she slipped from third place to fourth). Unlike Bedford's issue, that is an example of an injury that could not be overcome in time.

Again, triple jumper Jonathan Edwards was good but not great up to 1994. Then he contracted Epstein-Barr virus and was forced to rest. But at the World Championships in Gothenburg in 1995, he took his event to a whole new level, breaking the world record by huge margins with his first two jumps. In retrospect, his problem, like Bedford's but unlike Radcliffe's, was a blessing in disguise, enabling him to rest and reset.

So, your problem could be an injury, an illness (mental or physical), or in recent years, Covid-19. It could be a family bereavement, a personal crisis or work worry, which has naturally taken time, focus and emotional energy away from anything as trivial as running. It could be all manner of obstacles that life throws in our way.

And the 'it' that you fear to be out of reach, is usually a race, but could be something else, like a daily streak or a certain annual target of miles run.

Runners tend to fear the worst – or perhaps in some cases they subconsciously enjoy the excuse for not attempting a demanding goal! – so I tend to say, "Yes, of course you can still do it".

But, if you find yourself facing a setback (and who hasn't?), here are a few points to consider:

1. When you are in the middle of the problem, you need to strike the right balance between being kind to yourself and not expecting too much on the one hand, and on the other, doing what you can to prepare yourself for your return to training at the right time. When you are dealing with the core of the issue – for example, if a

relative has just died, or you have got Covid-19 – then you should obviously forget running and prioritise your and others' physical, mental and emotional well-being.

2. Later on, you may have the bandwidth to consider doing something more. When I am injured or ill, as I say, I always ask myself, "What can I do today to put myself in the best position to be able to return to running as soon as possible?" The answer could well be, "do nothing". But it could also be "go for a walk and then stretch", "have a massage or an ice bath", "foam roll", "do some strength training", "plan the next six months", "enter a race or two", "eat healthily", "do a 24-hour fast".

3. When you are recovering from physical or mental illness or injury, make sure you are back to good health before you do anything too strenuous. This takes objectivity – and a good coach can help here! Covid-19 has taught us that trying to return to active life too soon can be damaging, in the case of the pandemic leading to long Covid.

4. This next point may sound obvious – but it is something mentioned in every coaching manual, so it must need saying – don't attempt to take up where you left off before the problem emerged! Depending on the length of time out, you will probably have lost some fitness. In addition to this cardiovascular deficit, there is the structural dimension. Your legs – your knees, ankles and hips – will be less used to the impact of running. Give all of your bodily systems a gentle reintroduction to running. The human body is a marvellous instrument and can adapt to almost any demand – given the opportunity to build up gradually and sensibly.

5. Don't despair, you are definitely not starting from zero. All of the running and fitness work you have done in the past is still there, deep inside you – like the annual growth rings in the trunk of a tree. You may therefore find that, after two or three weeks of gentle running, you are suddenly moving a lot faster, or not feeling

so fatigued at the end of a session. This is still not the time to go all-out, but it is a positive indication that you are on the way back.

6. The rest is about common sense and self-monitoring, and being very honest with yourself about how you feel. You should still practise hard/easy days and weeks, ensuring that you have enough time to recover between meaningful efforts. At about this time, you can start to look at your original goal and decide if it is still feasible. Attempting a marathon on two weeks' training after six months out is not feasible. Attempting a marathon on six weeks' training after two months out may just be. But even that would need a finely judged build-up and almost certainly a revision of your time goal for the race.

Try not to be too disheartened if you are returning from illness or injury. You may just run better than before. Runners generally train too hard and run too much. History is littered with examples of great runners, like Bedford, logging massive mileages, getting injured and running their best times on their return – the injury providing the rest so sorely needed for them to achieve their fullest potential.

And do bear this in mind – runners almost never have the perfect build-up to their target race. But, by adopting a sensible schedule of hard and easy sessions, and managing to do **most** of the planned runs **most** weeks, you can achieve your aim.

CHAPTER 16
STAND – WHY SHOULDN'T I MAKE EXCUSES?

"This is an island. Here, you will die."

Nelson Mandela

AS A NAÏVE student starting out at Bristol University in 1976, I wondered what all the fuss was about. Why was the main bar in the Students' Union named after someone called Nelson Mandela?

It didn't take long for my more politically aware contemporaries to explain that fuss!

Mandela was then about halfway through a prison term that would only end in 1990 and would see him become a symbol of his nation's struggle against apartheid, as well as perhaps the most famous prisoner – maybe the most famous person – on the planet.

I've learnt a lot about the man since then. I greatly admire him. I expect we all do.

But something I learnt just recently has made me admire him in a whole new way.

Entering the prison on Robben Island, where he would spend 18 of his 27-and-a-half years in jail, a guard told him: "This is an island. Here, you will die."

Mandela, of course, responded to his imprisonment – and to this comment in particular – in many ways, but a major decision that he reached was that he must keep fit. He resolved that he would keep a connection with the boxing training that he had practised before his incarceration, when he used exercise to give himself physical and mental release from the frustrations of his daily political struggle.

And so that was what he did on Robben Island.

Even though the energy he had to do it with was drained by heavy manual labour, even though the space he had to do it in was just a 2.1 metre^2 cell, and even though the time he had available meant that he had to get up at 5am to fit it all in, he started to train.

He ran on the spot for 45 minutes; he did 100 press-ups on his fingertips; he completed 200 sit-ups; he executed 50 deep knee bends; and then he did various exercises borrowed from his previous boxing gym training, such as star jumps and burpees.

And then he went off to work all day in the quarry!

He did this every morning from Monday to Thursday, and then rested for three days.

This routine continued during his bouts of solitary confinement. It continued after his release. It naturally moderated with old age, but it never completely stopped until his death in 2013.

And we can all learn from Mandela's routine.

From a physical point of view, it was after all a good combination of cardiovascular endurance (the running) and a range of exercises that targeted pretty much all of the muscle groups.

But it did much more than have a merely physical effect.

From a mental and emotional perspective, he told reporters after his release that he found it absolutely essential to have something as an outlet for his anger. Like the punchbag in his activist days, his exercising provided that relief.

He also commented that the routine gave him serenity of mind. All the while the state was trying to break his spirit with hard labour, he was willingly putting his body through even more physical effort in order to prove to the authorities – and perhaps to confirm to himself – that their regime was not having the desired effect.

For that hour, four mornings a week, he was doing something that he – and he alone – had decided to do. And in that way, he was free.

But what does that mean for us?

Depending on our individual circumstances and responsibilities, the time that we have for ourselves may be limited or non-existent. Certainly, our time outside, away from our family, may be restricted. And the physical space that we have may also be constrained. The most extreme example of this was, of course, during the challenge of the Covid-19 lockdowns.

All of these difficulties are valid causes for concern, but there is surely a far more fundamental threat to our well-being. That threat is the temptation to let the situation, whatever its cause, control us completely – to decide that we cannot exercise, to decide that we cannot do anything for ourselves, to decide that we have no freedom.

To give up.

Albert Camus, the French-Algerian philosopher and writer, said: "The greatness of man lies in his decision to be stronger than his condition."

Nelson Mandela took the conscious decision to be stronger than the daily hard labour imposed by the government, to be greater than the confines of his tiny cell, to be freer than the bounds of his incarceration.

Whilst it may be an exaggeration to say that this decision alone set him on the path to becoming a greater political force and a stronger leader, I think that it was choices like this that amply demonstrated his belief system, that robustly shored up his sense of self-worth, and that ultimately empowered his premiership and enabled him to transform South Africa in the eyes of the world.

Although he was hemmed in on all sides and in all ways by the most horrendously difficult circumstances, he never gave up.

And neither should we.

The story of Nelson Mandela reminds us that we can always do something.

Now, my heart went out to those living in flats during the pandemic, or constrained by 24/7 childcare issues, but perhaps the following examples may give everyone some new ideas.

I'm not saying it's easy.

I think of Don Thompson preparing for the heat and humidity of the 1960 Rome Olympic Games (well before the days of Lottery-funded altitude or heat training camps, of course) by putting as many heaters as he could find in his bathroom and then exercising vigorously. (His wife once found him unconscious, but this turned out to be merely carbon monoxide poisoning rather than the rigours of his training!) He duly won gold in the 50km race walk.

I think of Emil Zátopek (four Olympic golds 1948–1952), a man so curious about the limits of human endurance that he trained almost constantly. Even on national service, on sentry duty, he ran on the spot and held his breath till he blacked out. When his wife, Dana Zátopková (also an Olympic gold medallist in javelin at the Helsinki 1952 Games), urged him to help a bit more around the house, he piled their dirty clothes into the bath with soap and water, and ran on them till he had pummelled them clean.

I think of Dorothy Tyler (nee Odam) (Olympic high jump silver medallist in 1936 and 1948) using her washing line for practice because there was no nearby track – and anyway she had to keep an eye on her children as they played in the garden.

I think of Ben Jipcho (Olympic silver medallist in the 1972 steeplechase) making his own barriers because his track in Kenya didn't have any – and making them several inches higher than the regulation 3ft, so that his training would be that much harder.

I think of Mal Whitfield (Olympic 800m champion 1948 and 1952, also on the 1948 4 x 400m gold-medal winning team) touring Africa and beating the native runners in informal races. When they pointed out that he had the advantage of proper running shoes whilst they ran barefoot, he simply took off his shoes and raced…and beat them again!

I think of the now disgraced and banned Alberto Salazar, number one marathon runner in the early 1980s, doing his 'callousing' sessions, running five miles in about 23 minutes, but running the test deliberately very early in the morning and also deliberately on a bumpy old cinder track rather than the modern tartan version that was also available to him.

I think of Ed Whitlock, the British-born Canadian, who set numerous world age bests in his seventies and eighties. (He was the oldest man ever, at 74, to break three hours for the marathon.) His case is pertinent because of the way he trained. He eschewed the beautiful trails within easy reach of his home and ran practically all of his miles around a cemetery. Building up to a marathon, he would run for three hours every day round the graves. Each lap took him just four minutes!

I think of David Hemery (Olympic gold medallist – 1968 400m hurdles, silver medallist – 1972 4 x 400m, and bronze medallist – 1972 400m hurdles) who trained through the Boston (USA) winters, with many a sand-dune session. "I liked the feeling of being able to put out everything I had, in every step of the dune sessions. It wouldn't be right for everyone, but for me, the hardest way was the best."[15]

As you know, I think of Ron Hill (European marathon champion in 1969 and Commonwealth marathon champion in 1970) who ran every day for over 52 years. He ran around airport lounges; he ran in his suit and work shoes when he had to; he 'ran' on crutches after an operation. But he ran. As he pointed out, his running streak meant that it was never a case of **if** he was going to run that day, but **when**, **where** and **how**.

15 *Another Hurdle*, David Hemery, page 146.

And I think of the training sequence in *Rocky IV* when our hero is preparing to face the Russian, Ivan Drago, who has killed Apollo Creed in the ring. The two men perform basically the same exercises, but, whilst Drago's are carried out in a state-of-the-art gym, Rocky's are performed in a barn in Siberia! When Drago does a push-press, Rocky presses a cart loaded with his trainer and family into the air. When Drago does a lateral power movement with weights, Rocky chops wood. And when Drago runs to exhaustion on an ever-elevating treadmill, Rocky runs up a mountain!

Cheesy I know, but it makes a point.

As you know, it doesn't really matter **what** you do, as long as you do something. The Rocky sequence is, of course, on YouTube. Maybe that could inspire you to do something? Watch out for Tony Burton, as Rocky's trainer, who died in 2016. When Rocky is holding agonising abdominal positions, Burton utters the immortal words, "No pain"!

Even during the Covid-19 lockdowns, runners challenged themselves to rise above the restrictions.

"I ate a lot of cocktail sausages on the way, so it's been a bit of a picnic really," said Carla Molinaro at the end of her record-breaking Land's End to John O'Groats run (often known as LEJOG). A picnic it most certainly wasn't, as Molinaro completed the roughly 874-mile journey in 12 days 0 hours 30 minutes and 14 seconds, from 16th–28th July 2020, breaking Sharon Gayter's 2019 record of 12:11:06:07. As is traditional – and rather wonderful – on these occasions, Sharon came out to support and encourage Carla during her run.

Molinaro ran and walked all through the last night to secure the record, battling headwinds, rain and generally atrocious conditions across the northernmost tip of Scotland. Even the guys accompanying her were exhausted at the end: "We've been out in this stuff all night, keeping her going," said one on video, indicating the storm outside the car window. "She's asleep in the other car now."

It seems that, with such a lot of races being cancelled during lockdown, many runners decided to pit their training against some classic challenges that did not require official approval to go ahead.

On 24th July 2020, Beth Pascall broke the women's record for the Bob Graham Round – the most famous challenge in fell running – a 66-mile, 42-peak journey with 26,900ft of ascent, which ordinary mortals try and complete within 24 hours. Beth took aim at Jasmin Paris's 2016 record of 15 hours and 24 minutes, succeeding with 14:34!!

On 16th July 2020, US ultra-runner John Kelly broke the record for the 268-mile Pennine Way with 2 days 16 hours 46 minutes, only for GB runner Damian Hall to better that eight days later with 2 days 13 hours 34 minutes. Before Kelly, Mike Hartley had held the record for 31 years with 2:17:20.

(I was lucky enough to share a lunch table with Hartley and Mike Cudahy at a GB Ultra squad weekend. Cudahy was Hartley's predecessor as record holder and the first man to run the Pennine Way in under three days. To say their conversation was fascinating is a huge understatement.)

Starting on 6th August 2020, Dan Lawson set a new men's record for the Land's End to John O'Groats run of 9 days 21 hours 14 minutes and 2 seconds. Well, I say new record…Guinness World Records for some reason recognises a time of 9 days and 2 hours by Andy Rivett from 2002, but, since his documentary evidence is very sketchy, he improved the record by such a huge margin and he never achieved anything else of note in ultra-running, no other expert believes him.

And on Sunday 2nd August 2020, someone called Harry Till completed his first marathon on a specially selected circuit between Medstead and Wield, west of Alton, Hampshire. His 26.3 (not 26.2) miles consisted of just over six circuits of 4.37 miles. Having run the first four laps in 37:51, 37:44, 37:11 and 38:40, he slipped to 42:48 on the fifth. Needing a last lap of 45 minutes or less for the sub-four-hour time he craved, he summoned all of his determination to complete it in 42:58, and then added another 38 seconds to reach 26.3 miles in 3:57:50, to be sure that he had reached at least the marathon distance.

If you challenge yourself in a way like this – and succeed – you will feel great. And then you really will deserve a cocktail sausage or two!

CHAPTER 17

SUPPORT – HOW CAN I SUPPORT A RUNNER?

"Are you sure you want to do this?"

SO YOU'RE MARRIED to or living with a runner, or you've fallen for one. Congratulations! In exchange for being involved with someone who is undoubtedly an awesome human being, whatever their sex or gender, there are some survival rules you've got to learn.

1. Don't call it jogging.
2. There will always be muddy shoes and sweaty kit around – possibly for days, probably not in the shoe rack and laundry basket.
3. Running shoes cost about the same as that weekend break you were hoping for. Don't be surprised which one they choose to spend their money on.
4. Of course, they need lots of pairs of running shoes! Haven't you got different outfits for different occasions?
5. The more expensive the running shoes, the less likely they are to get injured (they will tell you) – and you don't want them to get injured (see point 9).
6. Always have lots of food in the house and, if in doubt, over-cater.
7. You may have to wait a bit longer for that cosy night in on the sofa, if they haven't managed to fit a run in earlier that day.
8. If they haven't run, they will be grumpy. Which would you prefer – an evening of end-to-end grumpiness or a bit (OK, a lot – see point 10) less time with them?
9. If they are injured and can't run, best go away on holiday on your own for as long as you possibly can!
10. They will always be out for longer than advertised – the 'hour's run' they tell you about will be preceded by changing, stretching, checking the schedule, making sure all their gadgets are working, and a certain amount of faffing about (don't for goodness' sake say, "Are you sure you want to do this?"), it may itself be extended ("Thought I'd do some extra hills.") and will be followed by the warm-down, more stretching, a drink, an interminable time on something called a foam roller, a shower and then lots of painstaking record-checking, running log compiling and social media sharing.
11. Write off Sunday mornings.
12. Race day will be a nightmare. Accept it. The 'not a morning person' that you are used to will be transformed into this focused, intense, Type A psychopath. They will be so tense, you would think that they were entering some sort of *Hunger Games* or *Death Race 2000* instead of the local 10km.

13. You will not say the right thing. "Just enjoy it," is the wrong thing. "I'm sure you'll do well," is better but still not great. And, especially on race day, "Are you really sure you want to do this?" is grounds for the immediate cessation of the relationship.

14. During the event, if you are unlucky enough to encounter them out on the course, you will definitely not say the right thing. "Looking good," "Not far now," "Your teammate is just ahead," are all woefully inadequate and potentially explosive.

15. Afterwards, you cannot possibly say the right thing. If they've had a good race, they'll be incredibly irritating, and you won't be able to praise their time or position highly enough ("You just don't get what this means to me, do you?"). And if they haven't…well, just hope they have had a good race!

16. If you ever make the mistake of volunteering to support them in a long event, expect them never to be where you think they should be (or where they've said they would be – "Where on earth have you been?" tends not to go down too well in these circumstances), for you always to have the wrong drink/food/pair of socks/change of t-shirt ready for them, and point 14 still applies, but even more so. You are unlikely to live for very long after saying, "You look awful. Why don't you stop now?"

17. In the middle of races or runs, don't expect intelligent answers to your intelligent questions about what they want. A grunt is all you can expect…and you better interpret it correctly.

18. At the end, all you can do is ask them how it went – and then write off the next several hours as you receive a blow-by-blow account that makes the Terms and Conditions on your average bank account look like they were dashed off by an impatient apprentice who's late for the pub.

19. Try not to interrupt. What you optimistically perceive to be the end of the story will turn out to be the bit where they pause briefly for breath and say, "And then, in the second mile…"

20. Don't say, "Not *Chariots of Fire* again, love!"

21. Unless you actually have an eight-lane tartan track or cross-country course in your back garden, do not ask them to spend more time with you at home.

22. Holiday destinations will be chosen for their suitable running weather, running locations and range of running-related facilities. You will probably find that there just happens to be a race on in the next town the weekend you are there.

23. Always, and especially at the start of the relationship, try and avoid saying things like, "How many miles is the marathon you're doing?" or "But you went out yesterday," or "That teammate of yours has nice thighs," or "Can't you have dinner with me first?"

24. If you ever have to touch or, Lord help you, wash their kit, act as if you were restoring the Mona Lisa. Runners don't agree with capital punishment for many sins, but shrinking the club vest, or taking all the colour out of their favourite race t-shirt, are two of them.

25. If you happen to see their personal bests online, it's not a good idea to say, "That teammate of yours, you know, the one with the nice thighs, is two minutes faster than you".

26. Should you come to the end of your tether and decide on a "can't beat them, join them" approach, do **not**, under any circumstances, be faster than they are.

27. Never ever ask them to choose between running and you. There's always that person down the running club who understands them so much better than you do **and** has nice thighs.

28. Oh, and don't call it jogging.

Whilst we're talking about supporting your runner, you may wonder why this book is dedicated to Rod?

"You should have won," he said, after I'd come third in the 1985 Southampton Marathon. "Stupid to do so much last weekend. At one point, you were off the leaderboard. Stupid."

He didn't pull his punches, but then he had every right not to.

He'd ferried me to races before I could drive. He'd logged countless training runs alongside me. In the long ones, he'd stood for hours by the side of roads, and given me drinks and food. He'd coached me to where I was now.

And, to put it bluntly, I'd failed him.

I'd done too much, running up and down the sand dunes at Merthyr Mawr in South Wales the weekend before, when I should have been resting.

You won't have heard of Rod Lock, but then you won't have heard of the many thousands of people, just like him, up and down the country, who give so much of their time, effort, experience, intelligence and care, for the sheer love of their sport. The unsung heroes. And I'd like to use Rod's story to celebrate them all.

I've known Rod for a long time. Our interest in running really started when we both worked at Sainsbury's head office in the early 1980s. We encouraged each other, and a group of enthusiasts coalesced around Rod, as he encouraged us on regular 10-milers from the Blackfriars offices, along the embankment, through St. James's and Green Park, to do a lap of Hyde Park, before returning.

He planned excursions to the Sri Chinmoy Monday night races in Battersea Park and the London Road Runners Club (later Serpentine) Friday lunchtime 5kms in Hyde Park. Rod would organise teams for *The Sunday Times* Fun Run, as well as training weekends on the sand dunes of Merthyr Mawr, as the group got more serious. He also put together foreign trips to events such as the 20km de Paris and the Berlin Marathon.

Many Sainsbury's employees took up running – or simply did more – because of the supportive atmosphere that Rod had created.

Naturally, our excursions produced a few stories.

When he supported me with those drinks, we soon coined the mantra, "Not on a hill," as I found it difficult to swallow liquid when already breathing hard! When he once gave me a cup of water with some gravel in the bottom, I complained bitterly about the standard of service. Every subsequent time I asked for a drink, he would enquire: "With or without grit, Sir?"

We celebrated Rod's 40th birthday by running the New York City Marathon in 1989. Unfortunately, Rod stood a bit too close to the aerobics warm-up session before the start on Staten Island, and one lady's rather enthusiastic arm-thrust knocked the cup of hot chocolate he was holding all down his front, necessitating his running of the subsequent 26.2 miles in a rather uncomfortably sticky state!

We also did the 100th Boston Marathon in 1996. Oh, and much less importantly, he was Best Man at my wedding in 1988!

A lifelong Southampton resident and Saints fan, he was quick to lend his help to Southampton Athletics Club, where literally hundreds of athletes benefitted from his help over the years – from his detailed scientific schedules worked out individually and precisely for every athlete, to his occasional outbursts ("You're fired from my squad!").

Goodness only knows how many times he stood out on a freezing Southampton Common or by a rainy sports centre track, to shout splits to his athletes.

Members of the 'Rod Squad' set personal bests, won races and represented their country on numerous occasions, therefore it was deeply merited when the British Milers Club (the premier organisation for middle-distance running in the UK) awarded Rod their Lifetime Services to Coaching Award in 2022.

I don't think he ever realised quite how much difference he made to so many people over such a long period of time – but I hope and believe that award went some way towards persuading him of his outstanding contribution.

Because, for Rod, though he got to a very decent level of running himself, it was never about him. It was always about you. How were **you** doing? How was the injury? When was the next race? How fast were the kids now?

Rod battled cancer for decades. I remember visiting him in hospital way back – around 1990 – when he had had part of a lung removed. But he never made a big thing of it. It was a job for anybody to get a straight answer out of him – about what the surgeon had said, or even how he felt. It was never about him. It was always about you.

In 2022, the cancer got more aggressive and, having exhausted the possibilities of chemotherapy and radiotherapy, Rod was given the option of having some experimental treatment at the Royal Marsden Hospital in London.

He came out of hospital for Christmas and it is typical of the man that he was out in the woods, coaching a hill session on the 27th December. It is even more typical that, because one of his athletes couldn't make it on the 27th, Rod went out again on the 28th to supervise a solo session for them.

Unfortunately, he then reacted badly to the drugs, and his kidneys and liver shut down. He was rushed back into hospital early in January this year, but he soon deteriorated further.

The word went out, and it speaks volumes about the man that, on hearing of his condition on Facebook, so many of his runners dropped what they were doing and rushed to the ward. One 16-year-old, who had won her county cross-country championships that afternoon, insisted on her father driving her up to London so she could give her medal to Rod.

Even when we arrived, his main concern was that we had travelled so far to see him, and neglected our own needs!

Rod Lock crossed his last finish line at 8:55pm on 7th January 2023, aged 73.

No words of mine can really do justice to the decades-long, multifaceted nature of the help, support, advice and service that he gave so freely to so many.

A great coach, a great laugh, a great friend, simply a great human being.

I was honoured to speak at Rod's funeral on 26th April 2023, organised so beautifully by Matt Bennett and Matt Hibberd, alongside Mick Varley, and members of the Rod Squad, including Gareth Klepacz, Nigel Wright, Matt Hibberd, Matt Revier and Alex Teuten.

We probably all know someone like Rod. I, for one, will certainly make sure to thank them when I see them, while they are still around to be thanked. I hope you will too.

RIP Rod – and thanks for all the grit!

CHAPTER 18

GIVE – IS PARKRUN FOR ME?

"They were cheering me. ME!"

KATHY NEVER THOUGHT that running or jogging was for her – let alone something as organised as parkrun. This is her story.

"I got divorced five years ago. The kids had left home and, to be honest, I really struggled. I ate too much. I'd never really exercised regularly – you know, the odd class at the gym, and a bit of walking, but nothing with any routine.

Not surprisingly, I put on weight, and it started to get me down. I was puffed out just walking upstairs.

Then I saw on Facebook that one of my friends, Julie, had done something called parkrun, and apparently had got a t-shirt. The next time I bumped into her, I asked her about it.

Well, I couldn't shut her up! It was the best thing ever. It was the highlight of her week. It had changed her life!

She asked me if I wanted to come along. I said no, I wasn't nearly fit enough to consider doing something like that.

She said anyone was fit enough to come along and walk round. She made me promise to go home and register, and to think about it.

Less than an hour later, she called me. Had I registered? No, I hadn't! Right, she was coming round!

We sat and she registered me, and she showed me some pictures on the website from the previous week. Some of the people doing parkrun actually looked normal! They looked a bit like me – but happier!

"I'll pick you up at 8:15am on Saturday," she said, walking out of the front door, without giving me the chance to say no.

And so it was that I went to my first parkrun.

I was terribly nervous. There were people already running around. They all looked very fit. But everyone was very friendly.

Julie stood with me at the 'first timers' briefing'. It all seemed quite straightforward, but I was still so nervous.

Wisely, looking back, Julie had taken me to a parkrun with two equal laps.

She stood with me at the back of the line-up of runners, joggers and walkers. It felt like the Olympic final!

Luckily, the course was flat. We set off. I noticed that we had two people in hi-vis just behind us – I later learned that they were called the Tail Walkers.

The first 10 minutes or so were OK, but then the fast runners came streaming past me, and that really put me off. But, amazingly, quite a few of them gave us words of encouragement.

Julie had brought a bottle of water, and that helped.

Before too much longer, we could see the end of the first lap, and I was more than ready to stop.

I was as red as a beetroot, out of breath, so tired, very glad to sit down in the café, but also a little bit pleased with myself.

Julie, bless her, stayed with me, not carrying on to complete her second lap. I did enjoy that coffee!

She took me home, helping me out of the car and through the front door – oh, the indignity of it all!

There then came a difficult episode of trying to crawl upstairs, peel off my leggings and get into and out of the shower.

Again, wisely, Julie left it till the next Tuesday to call me. "How do you feel now?"

I said I was really pleased with myself for doing as much as I did, but I'd never do a whole parkrun.

"Let's go for a walk tomorrow," she said.

OK.

So, we walked for half an hour on the Wednesday. We did the first lap of parkrun again that Saturday. I walked with Julie the next Tuesday, and on my own on the Thursday.

That Saturday, I told Julie I had the confidence to do the first lap on my own, and for her to go off and do the two laps.

This continued for another couple of weeks, and then something strange happened. We were driving to parkrun.

"Julie, I, er, I want to do the whole thing."

I don't really know why those words suddenly came out of my mouth. "Great," said Julie.

We lined up at the back, as usual. We set off nice and slowly, but this time we got a bit further round the first lap before the sprinters passed us.

At the end of the first lap, I could smell the coffee being served in the café, and I was tempted to stop, but…

Once we were out of 'tempting smells' range, it was a bit easier. I got really tired in the middle of the second lap, but Julie – bless her once again – supplied me with water and encouragement, and before too long, we were in sight of the finish.

I was going to finish my first parkrun!

And then, a second strange thing happened.

I began to jog.

Nothing spectacular, you understand, and I must have looked pathetic, but I was actually jogging for the first time in years.

And then the third strange thing…

All of the finish marshals, the timekeepers, the two Tail Walkers behind us – and quite a few of the guys who had already finished – started applauding and cheering.

They were cheering me. **ME!**

I couldn't help it. I started crying. I sobbed on Julie's shoulder for a fair old time once we'd crossed the finish line, and all I could blurt out was, "Thank you, Julie, thank you, thank you".

I looked at my finish token in disbelief. I had it scanned. And the gentleman scanning it said "well done".

We walked into the café, and all the people at the tables we passed said "well done".

Blooming heck, even the girl behind the counter making the coffee said "well done"!

And oh, it tasted good!

A couple of hours later, I looked at the results on the website – and I started crying again!

Just as it had done with Julie, parkrun had changed my life.

Fast-forward from there, I managed to get my red 50 t-shirt just before lockdown – just after Julie got her black 100 one – and I've also done a couple of 10km races.

And perhaps more importantly, parkrun gave me the reason, the motivation, the habit and the self-belief to keep exercising all through lockdown, so once parkrun returned, I was there and I was ready."

Well done, Kathy.

So, is parkrun for **you**?

Well, let me say this. I have seen squaddies run parkrun in army boots and a full pack. I have seen hen parties hula hoop round the entire 5km! I know of one parkrunner whose terminal cancer has meant that he can now no longer complete the distance by any means, but who volunteers every week at a stationary marshal point. And I know of a parkrun in London, where the neighbouring care home staff wheel one old lady, in her chair, to a corner of the course every week – come rain or shine – where she receives a (very gentle) high five from every single runner as they pass.

Of course parkrun is for you!

CHAPTER 19

TRACK – WHAT DOES IT ALL MEAN?

"I was resting on billowy white clouds that would, I thought, then, always protect me from the worst of life's buffetings."[16]

Roger Bannister, third from left, starts the first four-minute mile

SO SAID ROGER Bannister after running the first sub-four-minute mile.

---

16 *First Four Minutes*, Roger Bannister, page 194.

I believe that he felt this because he had achieved a feat that he could always look back on with great pride, because he had done something meaningful.

Bannister's is a powerful statement, because it suggests that doing one thing – admittedly, a 'thing' that he had devoted a large part of his physical, mental and emotional life to over several years – could actually be life-defining, could outweigh whatever negativity occurred elsewhere in his time on earth.

How do we look at our lives? Or, to put it another way, what do we need in life? What do we need in order to reach Bannister's point of nirvana? And indeed, is it available to ordinary mortals, or can it only be reached by someone, like Bannister, who runs the first four-minute mile, composes a symphony that will be played for evermore, or discovers a cure for cancer?

What do we ordinary mortals need in life? Happiness? Enjoyment?

Enjoyment? But is enjoyment meaningful without achievement?

"I've won the lottery." Is that meaningful? I mean you didn't do anything to deserve it. You didn't 'achieve' it, in any meaningful sense.

"I've made my bed." Is that meaningful? Well, I mean it wasn't hard.

"I've been for a run." Is that meaningful? Hmm.

"I've set a PB." Is that meaningful? Maybe.

John Stuart Mill, commonly acknowledged as the most influential English philosopher of the 19th century, at one point in his life started to analyse whether he was happy – and promptly had a mental breakdown. Later, he concluded that you couldn't achieve happiness by making it your primary aim: "Those only are happy, who have their minds fixed on some object other than their own happiness; on the happiness of others, on the improvement of mankind, even on some art or pursuit, followed not as a means, but as itself an ideal end. Aiming thus at something else, they find happiness by the way."

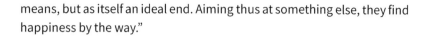

With all of that in mind, let's look at running through the prism of those thoughts, in the context of the rest of our lives.

Sometimes in winter, when I am running across the frozen fields, I will get really cold and start to feel sorry for myself. Then I remember Stalingrad – I wasn't there, you understand, but Antony Beevor's book of that name evokes the suffering of both sides so vividly that you almost believe that you are indeed out there on the Russian steppe.

The 1942–1943 battle for the city, now known as Volgograd was fought in temperatures that reached minus 40 degrees. When the Germans finally surrendered, the Soviets kept their prisoners of war (POW) in simple rings of wire – no huts, no tents, no shelter and little winter clothing. Beevor says that at night they had to stand together in threes or fours, with a blanket over their heads to keep their warm breath in, trying to sleep, "like horses".

It is notoriously difficult to establish how many of the prisoners died, but many records put the total number of Germans taken prisoner by the Soviets in the Second World War at three million, with around one million dying. Contrast this with the estimated fate of the Sixth Army who surrendered at Stalingrad, where, of 91,000 original prisoners, only 6,000 made it back to their home country. To me it seems miraculous, given the savage conditions in which they were kept, that any survived at all.

And so I think, out there on Windmill Hill in the winter of southern England, no, this is not really that cold.

One Sunday back in the summer of 2022, I watched my son run the Richmond Park Half Marathon in (plus) 35 degrees. His target of a new personal best lasted for a few miles before the reality of what David Coleman would have called "torrid conditions" kicked in.

And my thoughts turned from my son to my father, who died 12 years ago. After years out in Burma in the RAF during the war, he could not stand any real heat – and he didn't really want to be away from his home either. We never had a proper summer holiday because of that insecurity and because the glare of the sun reminded him physically – but also now looking back, probably more deeply emotionally – of those desperate years in the Far East.

So I thought, watching my son sweat round Richmond Park, no, this is not really that hot!

My thoughts turn to when I had a couple of teeth extracted. I was in the dentist's chair for an hour and a half as she pulled and wrenched and drilled and levered, joking that, with all this exercise, she wouldn't need to go to the gym that night – oh, how, for many reasons, I didn't laugh! It was worse when the anaesthetic wore off. I felt pretty sorry for myself then too.

But then I thought of my friend, Guy.

Immediately I extracted myself from my little world of woe and tried to inhabit the mind of a man with terminal cancer who is in constant and intense physical pain – exacerbated by the mental anguish of not knowing how long he will be there for his family. And yet here is a man, who, if you met him, would come across as the most positive, engaging, sociable and happy person.

He was given an absolute maximum of five years to live – five and a bit years ago. Now, the 'bit' is significant, because the one last thing he wanted to live to see was his younger daughter graduate with her veterinary degree.

And one Saturday some time ago, he did.

There he was in the photos on Facebook, with his arm round his daughter in her gown, Guy wearing her mortarboard and laughing. One can only guess the depth of emotion for all concerned behind those smiles.

Guy is the bravest person I have ever met – with the possible exception of my Mum, who, when **she** was in the dentist's chair, refused to have injections for a filling: "I'd much rather have a bit of discomfort for a few minutes than that awful numb feeling for hours afterwards."

My Mum also had Parkinson's disease for the last 30 or so years of her life, and in one meeting with her consultant, discussing her deteriorating condition, she said: "Oh well, there are lots of people worse off than me."

"Yes," he replied, "but that doesn't help you now, does it, my dear?"

She thought that was a lovely thing for him to say, and, I guess, in the circumstances, it was. This memory makes me reconsider, once again, my weak and woebegone self – cold in a wintry field, sore post-extraction – and reminds me that it is sometimes instructive to extract oneself from one's immediate concerns and scan, for a moment, the wider context of all human bravery and endurance.

It also makes me ponder anew why we run.

It can't just be to keep fit, can it? If it were just that, why wouldn't we do something more 'pleasurable' that involves kicking or hitting a ball towards a hole, a goal or a boundary rope, something more 'productive' with more of a tangible outcome?!

Sport has been called the modern alternative to war. And, with all due deference to the wars still raging across the globe, certainly, during the Second World War, my father – and my mother – knew what life was all about, understood the meaning of their roles and grasped the point of their existence.

It humbles me to think of their wartime lives. As Edgar says at the end of William Shakespeare's *King Lear*, "The oldest hath borne most; we that are young / Shall never see so much, nor live so long".

In the absence of war, which gave our parents and grandparents such an obvious purpose in life, isn't running something of a substitute for that today?

I am not saying that we don't live to raise our children – "No, don't go for a personal best in this heat, son!" – and pursue a career, and be kind to our friends and neighbours, but the human spirit, in my view, is constantly searching for truer and deeper meaning.

And running can sometimes be one of the few things that offers this.

I certainly know that, some days, when work has been frustrating and family relations strained, the only thing that really makes any sense is going for a run.

I am not for one minute suggesting that pounding the mean streets of Alton lets me share in the suffering of my father in Burma, of Guy's cancer, of my mother's Parkinson's, or of those German POWs, for goodness' sake.

But, whilst acknowledging the disgraceful but very real need for initiatives such as foodbanks in 21st century Britain, for those of us lucky enough to exist in a fairly comfortable, insulated, airconditioned and well-upholstered world, let's face it, day-to-day life can be a bit dull.

So, the solitary and seemingly selfish act of running can reduce our lives, as few other things can, to the basic elements of time and space, cold and heat, energy and fatigue, pain and endurance, and thereby ironically (given its selfish image) nurture a greater fellow feeling (why else would otherwise extremely competitive endurance athletes support each other in the white heat of battle?), a stronger connection to the universe, and, forgive my romanticising, a chance to glimpse perhaps a little more of the meaning of life.

As Haruki Murakami, author of *What I Talk About When I Talk About Running*, said: "As I run, I feel that's not all there is to it. There's something more important deeper down in running."

And, as Adharanand Finn, author of *Running With The Kenyans*, said: "If we push on, we begin to feel a vague, tingling sense of who, or what, we really are."

CHAPTER 20

OLDER – AM I TOO OLD (OR YOUNG) TO START?

"When I saw myself in the photos of my daughter's wedding, I knew I needed to do something about my weight."

Brian after the Havant Half Marathon

SO SAID BRIAN. He was 50 at the time. He started jogging. No set schedule, no real goals, just a few miles when and where he could.

And the amazing thing was, he was a natural. He sometimes ran with his aforementioned daughter, who had herself been running for many years, but he was soon outpacing her.

Within a couple of months, he had done his first race, the Victory 5 Mile in Portsmouth. The next year, he worked up from the Eastleigh 10km (pacing his daughter) and the Great South Run (10 miles) to a half marathon! Quite remarkable progress. But that's not all, because he had another reason for running.

His wife had severe arthritis and, in some of his races, Brian raised funds for Arthritis Research UK (now Versus Arthritis), posting the following on his employer's bulletin board before one half marathon:

> *I run for myself most of the time,*
> *Along roads, down paths, up hills.*
> *And while I run and while I climb,*
> *I give thanks I have no ills.*
>
> *But sometimes when I run along,*
> *I think of those less fit.*
> *Whose arms and legs are not so strong,*
> *Makes me want to help a bit.*
>
> *And so in March, I'll run the 'half',*
> *Thirteen miles of slog.*
> *The first hour's always quite a laugh,*
> *But it isn't just a jog.*
>
> *More important, though, than how I feel,*
> *Is what I aim to achieve.*
> *I'll be raising cash for the arthritis appeal,*
> *With every footprint I leave.*

So please sponsor me now for my charity run,
From five pence to five pounds a mile.
I'll be donating the sweat and the grunts,
You'll give others a reason to smile.

In later years, heart problems slowed him and eventually brought an end to his running career, but he kept his medals and his memories – and the odd picture of himself powering towards another race finish line.

So, what lessons can we draw from Brian's story? Perhaps, most importantly, that it's never too late to start. That you should run as you feel. Enjoy it. Compete if you want. Be grateful for every run and every race. And run for others if you can. Brian would be proud of passing on those thoughts.

Brian Nash was my father-in-law, and it was at my wife's and my wedding in 1988 that he recognised that he was in need of exercise. In subsequent years, the three of us shared many miles and even more smiles.

Brian died in January 2021, crossing his final finish line, and at his funeral, as well as tributes to his many other gifts, another poem reminded us of his love of running:

Not many of you know – and this is a stunner –
That Brian was actually a very good runner.

When he saw the photos from his daughter's wedding,
He said: "There's some pounds there, I should be shedding."

"I'll do some running, like my daughter."
And he took to it, like a duck to water.

In just two months, he began to thrive,
With a classy performance at the Victory 5.

Six months later, he was up to 10 miles,
The Nash legs pounding, the face all smiles.

The very next year, he was doing the half,
Thirteen miles? He was having a laugh.

And he was always so supportive, let me say that with clarity,
Raising money for arthritis charities.

And I bet he's now running round heaven's sunlit campus,
With all the family dogs, from Roni to Trampas.

RIP Brian

Another story…

On 27th October 2014, my daughter, Gabriella, ran a mile round the field at the back of our house, and changed my life.

You see, she got me wondering. I should be able to do that, I thought.

I am going to share the story of how I got back into running, in the hope that it will help you.

Let me give you a bit of context. I had been a runner since 1971, but, since early 2010, when my left knee went dodgy and my right foot quickly followed suit, I had only really run in parkruns, not training at all during the week.

Inevitably, I had lost fitness, put on weight, got slower, lost more fitness, put on more weight – to the point where I could just about squeeze out a sub-30-minute time on a very flat parkrun, but my (hilly) Alice Holt parkrun times were typically 33–35 minutes.

So, on that beautiful autumn morning in 2014, I went out into the field and slogged my way round – slowly, tentatively, painfully – but at the end, I was smiling, I was glowing, and I felt like a runner, like an athlete, for the first time in nearly five years.

After that – well, you know how it is – one thing led to another. I ran two miles the next day. Then a bit more. I started eating a bit more healthily. And suddenly, I was running 31 minutes at Alice Holt parkrun, then 29. These weekly boosts of confidence inspired me to run more, add speedwork, stretch, do more in the gym – and eat more intelligently too. My knee and my foot stopped me from running more than three or four times a week, but I was doing everything else I could to get faster.

On non-running days, I would race walk uphill as fast as I could, hoping to boost my metabolic rate without stressing my joints. I started rowing for half an hour on every gym visit – soul-destroying but body-enhancing, I called it. I made small dietary changes – Americanos instead of lattes, porridge instead of buttery toast, salad instead of crisps and dips, chicken tikka instead of chicken tikka masala.

And I had discovered, almost by accident, the perfect virtuous weekly circle of running more often, eating more healthily, getting fitter and seeing my times improve, which then gave me the motivation to carry it all on the following week. (The weekly challenge of parkrun was crucial to keeping that momentum.)

It felt great. I did improve almost every week. It was exciting. I didn't know how far I'd get, but I thought if I could just set one more Alice Holt parkrun PB (it was 28:21 back then), I could die a happy man!

Well, having set 10 more Alice Holt PBs and many more at other parkruns too, I am at the point where I am doing 23 minutes for a flat parkrun and am down to 24:51 at my beloved Alice Holt. I have also run longer races, even slogged round a marathon. I **even** won a (handicap) race; I **even** overtook a certain Harry Till at Alice Holt once. My lead over him was temporary, but no less jubilant for that!

That October morning had indeed changed my life.

So, I want to say to you all – young or old, fit or not quite so fit – if Brian can do it, if I can do it, can turn it around, then you can too. Make small changes – to your diet and your exercise routine – do a bit more than you have been. Be patient; try and be consistent; don't despair if you slip back; but give it a bit of time, and you will start to notice the changes – in your shape, in your stamina, in your speed.

Exercise-wise, I've been up and I've been down – and I know where I prefer to be. And if I can't convince you, maybe David Ginola can – you're worth it!

———————————————

"You know, we used to be good," I said to the other old guy at the back of the field towards the end of the Alton 10km.

He came right back at me.

"We're as good as we ever were, Steve. We're out here and we're giving all we've got. It hurts just as much as ever, doesn't it? Maybe we're not as fast as we were. And maybe we don't look as smooth, but there ain't no prizes for style in running. We are just doing it. And that's all that counts."

And he was right.

There is something noble about the ageing athlete (in any sport, except perhaps, for obvious reasons, boxing) who takes Dylan Thomas's words to heart:

Do not go gentle into that good night.
Rage, rage against the dying of the light.

A typical cross-country race I ran in recently was a case in point – full of 40, 50, 60 and 70-year-olds and possibly older, still out there in the mud and the hills, not just plodding round, but competing strenuously against their peers, fighting for every place and every second. Somehow, I don't think they'll ever retire.

Roger Mills, European bronze medal-winning race walker, said: "When they nail me down, I'll be thinking about the next race."

Some, of course, do retire early. Herb Elliott, Olympic 1,500m champion in Rome in 1960, double Commonwealth champion, world record holder at 1,500m and the mile, and unbeaten over those distances in his entire senior career, retired at 22. Perhaps he felt he had no more peaks left to climb.

Daley Thompson, on the other hand, after Olympic decathlon golds in 1980 and 1984, and a heart-breaking fourth in 1988 (losing the bronze medal in the last of the 10 events), attempted to qualify for Barcelona 1992 at the age of 33. He pulled up injured halfway through the first event of the 10, the 100m.

When questioned by the press afterwards about the futility of an attempt to qualify that only lasted five seconds instead of two days, Thompson responded characteristically: "Ah, but what a five seconds it was!"

Do we admire Elliott because he knew exactly when to retire, or Thompson because he didn't know when to give up?

My sympathy is with the stayer.

Of course, age doesn't have to mean deceleration or decline. Derek Turnbull, the sheep farmer from Invercargill, New Zealand, hardly lost a step all his running life. As I've said, I trained with him round his home farm tracks in early 1992 and witnessed (sometimes from afar!) exactly how hard he ran. And how much rich dairy food he consumed!

A couple of months later, in **my** home city of London, he set a world age record for the marathon of 2:41:57. He was 65-years-old.

But most of us do struggle more as the years go by. I bumped into Tony Simmons recently (silver medallist in the 1974 European 10,000m, fourth in the 1976 Olympic Games). He said he gave up racing when he couldn't break 32 minutes for 10km anymore!

At a very different level, a little while ago, I ran a track mile at a speed that, 20 years ago, I could maintain for 100km. But, as my friend in the Alton 10km said, it felt just as hard, and it was all I could give at the time.

So when I see a runner out there on the streets of Alton, or the beautiful trails around Hampshire, and I see that they're not as young as they were, and they're limping a bit because maybe they've got a bad knee or an arthritic foot, but they're still out there, I can't help but smile and silently applaud.

Well, I have been known to loudly applaud!

And I would say to you, whatever your age, if you are running, keep at it. And if you're not, give it a go. Running is weight-bearing, so, yes, the knees and the ankles take a bit of a pounding, but, if you get the right shoes and you build up sensibly, then the pounding is actually an additional benefit (not available to cyclists or swimmers) because it's great for your bone density and protecting yourself against fractures as the years go by.

Incidentally, it's wonderful for your body, mind and spirit too!

Once again: for those older athletes just starting out, I would urge you to consider parkrun, where crucially the prizes (t-shirts for 25, 50, 100, 250, etc. runs) are given to those who keep on running, rather than those who finish first.

The trick, of course, is to keep pushing the envelope without going too far. I'll never now run another marathon or half marathon – it's just too much for my knees to take – but I will keep doing the 10kms and the five-mile cross-country races, because, if I didn't and just limited myself to 5kms, pretty soon that's all I'd be **able** to do. Use it, or you will lose it.

And if you can get out there and discover that runner's high (at least in retrospect!) then a fire will be lit inside you that will warm, guide and inspire you for the rest of your life. As Samuel Beckett said:

"Perhaps my best days are gone…but I wouldn't want them back, not with the fire in me now."

I suppose while we're at it, we should ask if you are ever too **young** to start? Let me answer that question in this way:

"Hey, Sam, we're running up the dragon's neck."

"No, we're not, Dad. Don't be silly."

"Where are we then?"

"We're on the dragon's bum!"

Dragon Hill is a major feature of Alice Holt parkrun, so named because, well, it does drag on, because by halfway up it we're all breathing fire, and finally because, in that remote corner of the forest, we think there may well actually be dragons.

Sam was enjoying the run with his Dad, and it was great to hear his perky enthusiasm. And whilst his Dad didn't get their location exactly correct, what he did get right was that he was making the run not a chore, but an adventure for his little boy.

Let me share another couple of comments overheard at parkrun.

"OK, Ben – let's walk this bit – I'm a bit tired."

"Come on, Hattie, own the hill. Don't let the hill own you."

These are two examples of parents 'encouraging' their children. It perhaps won't surprise you to learn that little Ben was smiling and enjoying the whole experience of running and walking with his Dad, whereas Hattie was on the verge of tears the entire time. (Names have been changed to protect the guilty.)

People ask me, should children run? My answer is, always, if **they** want to. Watch children in the playground – when they are playing games, they run as fast as they can, and then they stop, then they go again. Kids are built for intermittent effort; they're not designed for the steady grind of a non-stop 5km.

And yet, time and again, I see mothers and fathers trying to get their children to keep running when they should be walking, or doing 5km when they should be doing 2km.

Ben's Dad got it right – he didn't even wait until his son said he was tired; he gave his boy the reason to stop and walk.

Whilst it is tempting for an adult tasked with childcare on a Saturday morning and who wants to complete another parkrun, to persuade their child to do the whole 5km, that may not be in the child's best interests. In fact, it may put them off running for a very long time.

For some of these reasons, and many others, parkrun have introduced junior parkruns on Sunday mornings. They are 2km (not 5km), for 4–14-year-olds (though responsible adults can participate alongside the children), and they are totally marshalled. That means that all participants are within sight of a marshal at all times.

What a great initiative! And the website makes it clear that, whilst some athletes may want to race these events, the key focus is for everyone to have fun in a safe environment.

You only have to read some of the comments in the news section of the junior parkrun website to understand how completely the kids themselves 'get' this ethos – they talk about supporting others, playing in the playground afterwards, making friends, not worrying about times (even relishing a new 'personal worst'), eating cake and just doing it.

Of course, running is not the only sport for youngsters. I would encourage all children to try out a range of games. My own son tried football, and then rugby, before realising his vocation lay in hockey – with a bit of running on the side to keep him fit!

Even within athletics, there are the jumps, the throws and the hurdles, in addition to sprints and endurance running.

Running is **not** for everyone; but everyone can find a sport that is right for them.

That is why I say, "Let them run if they want to". It is so important to empower the children to decide for themselves whether they want to run or not, how far and how fast they want to go, when they want to walk and when they want to stop altogether.

And make it an adventure for them: after all, it's not every day that you get to run on a dragon's bum!

CHAPTER 21

MENTAL – HOW STRONG IS MY MIND?

"I'm not really that mentally strong."

Ronnie O'Sullivan

WHEN 'THE ROCKET' Ronnie O'Sullivan won his seventh World Snooker Championship in 2022, equalling Stephen Hendry's record, my mind went back to an interview he had given after one of his earlier triumphs.

When asked how many more titles he thought he could win, he claimed that he really wasn't that mentally strong – in the way that Ray Reardon and Steve Davis were strong – and that he might be able to win one or two more, but that he just couldn't keep doing it year after year.

What has this got to do with running?

Well, you see, my mind also went back to his 2013 autobiography (written with Simon Hattenstone), where he gave all the credit for getting him in the right frame of mind to win back-to-back championships in 2012 and 2013 – while hardly even competing between them – to running.

Indeed, the book is simply called, *Running*.

Running had given him the mental strength he had been lacking.

Now, one has to set Ronnie's triumphs against a personal background that he has been quite open about, and that he would admit has been unsettling, to say the least. His father was convicted of murder when Ronnie was still an adolescent; he doesn't see his first child; he is divorced from the mother of his other two children and has struggled to gain access to them from time to time; and he has been addicted to drugs and alcohol for periods of his career.

All of this has naturally interfered with his ability to focus on his snooker. But, slowly but surely, he found running.

And he began to recognise that he felt better – and crucially played better – when he was running-fit.

And pretty fit he was too!

He ran 35 minutes for 10km, trained with some international runners and at one time harboured ambitions to make the Essex cross-country team. But, more than this, he liked the fact that his running mates didn't talk about snooker. He liked being out in the open air. And he talked about running being his therapy, the main staple of his life, cleansing him through its healthy pain.

Because, when he first hit the scene, the signs were that he would not last long. He could shoot a maximum break – and then shoot his mouth off. The fans loved him, but it was obvious that he was fragile, brittle – a John McEnroe rather than a Roger Federer, a George Best not a Bobby Charlton, more Ayrton Senna than Jackie Stewart.

But his addiction to running replaced the aforementioned, more dangerous obsessions, and he won the World Championship in 2001, 2004, 2008, 2012, 2013, 2020 and 2022, becoming the oldest player to lift the trophy.

Winning his seventh world title meant that Ronnie's championship record matched his place in his supporters' hearts. His objective record had caught up with his subjective legend, if you like. His success justified the fans' belief that he is the greatest (most talented) player ever – witness those 15 maximum breaks (clearing all of the balls in one visit to the table for a score of 147), the fastest being in a mind-boggling five minutes eight seconds (YouTube it!).

Fans had feared that his record might resemble those other two great natural talents – and natural entertainers – Alex 'Hurricane' Higgins (two titles) and Jimmy 'Whirlwind' White (six times a losing finalist – in 1984 and, incredibly, every year from 1990 to 1994).

Indeed, the somewhat up and down nature of his career is put into perspective by the fact that, rather than the 2001–2022 span it took Ronnie, Hendry won all of his seven world titles in the years from 1990 to 1999.

In applauding O'Sullivan's triumph – and celebrating his turning his life around – we can all empathise with his view of running as cleansing, a healthy pain, can't we?

Who of us has not had a personal tragedy, turmoil or trial that has been ameliorated by the simple act of going for a run?

The loss of a loved one, say, does not disappear during a run, but despair can be replaced by something a little more positive or useful. We may step out of the door, just hoping to run away from reality, as it were, but the outing can unconsciously move us in a different direction – becoming a sort of tribute to the lost person perhaps, a meditation on their place in our heart, and possibly a journey of catharsis.

On a far more trivial level, who of us has not started a run with a problem nagging away in our minds and ended it with the solution – without even having thought about it during the intervening miles?!

And negative emotions – anger, regret, resentment – can often vanish, or at least fade and find their proper dimensions, during a run.

Running is unique in this, I think. Perhaps the same could be said for cycling, swimming or walking, but one would not immediately think of trying to come to terms with the loss of a loved one by, say, playing a game of tennis or a round of golf – or a frame or two of snooker!

There is something about the simplicity of a run, the fact that you can do it alone, with the minimum of equipment or preparation, and that you don't have to think about it or think during it.

And then there is the effect of the regular rhythmic stride, with every footfall being at the same time identical and different, if you will.

Without getting too zen about it all, many people have claimed that running is meditative, hypnotic or that it at least can be mindful – and science has shown us that it slows the release of stress hormones (adrenalin and cortisol), whilst increasing that of endorphins – the brain's feel-good neurotransmitters, giving us that 'runner's high'.

Amid the turbulence of considerable personal pain and public pressure in his early career, Ronnie O'Sullivan was no doubt drawn instinctively towards running by those very factors. And we should all be grateful that its lifelong benefits have seen him finally fulfil his talent and claim his rightful place at the very top of his sport's roll of honour.

CHAPTER 22
BELIEVE – WHY CAN'T I GIVE UP?

"My knee really hurt on the tempo run today."

THE FINISH LINE clock ticked mercilessly towards '02:11:00'. Her personal best was 2:11:51, and she was nowhere in sight. I was worried a PB was out of reach. But suddenly, there she was, knees and arms driving, and a look on her face that said: 'I'm not going to miss it now!'

And indeed, she didn't – official time, 2:07:07.

Like an idiot, her coach (me!), in my rush to see her just after the race began, had completely forgotten that it must have taken her a few minutes to cross the start line.

To achieve such a great result, it had been a long road, and not a smooth one either.

I hope that her story is a useful example of how one can reap extremely satisfying rewards, firstly by designing a training schedule, secondly by sticking to it, thirdly by revising it if the unexpected happens, and then finally by "executing your race plan" (as Michael Johnson would say) on the day.

Having run the London Marathon in October 2021, this athlete set her sights on revising her shorter distance personal bests, with the half marathon first up, so together we concocted a plan.

Alongside two gym sessions during the week and an easy parkrun on Saturdays, she would build up the distance of a longer run on the Sundays, starting at around six miles and culminating at 11 two weeks before this target race – the Southampton Half Marathon.

She would also complete two more demanding sessions on Tuesdays and Thursdays. Tuesdays would be tempo sessions; Thursdays would be hill sprints of varying distances, or flat efforts with limited recovery.

We felt that the tempo runs were particularly important, designed to raise her cruising pace to the required level.

Her half marathon personal best was almost exactly 10-minute miles, and a three-mile run at that speed was her initial limit, so we built up from three separate miles at 9:30, to two continuous miles at 9:00, and so on, eventually to four miles non-stop at 8:30.

We knew that it was essential, in a 13.1-mile race, for her to feel that the required sub-10 pace was easy in the initial miles, doable in the middle section, and still within her determined compass towards the end.

We also believed that her long runs would provide the endurance to continue said effort over the whole distance, and that the hills and flat efforts would supply the leg strength and raw speed to make the target pace viable.

Training seriously for an event like this, as I have said, has to be multi-layered in this way. It is about working on all of your 'gears' in the different sessions, so that, on race day, the speed, strength, speed-endurance and sheer stamina all come together to give the athlete the best possible opportunity to deliver an optimum performance.

Now this athlete is very conscientious. Obedient would also be an appropriate word – something coaches always appreciate in a runner!

Every Sunday night, she would send me feedback on the previous seven days.

MONDAY. Gym.
TUESDAY. One warm-up / aim three @ 9:30, did 9:24, 9:20, 9:29, felt good / one warm-down.
WEDNESDAY. Gym; did the optional easy three miles too.
THURSDAY. One warm-up / hills: 2 x 15 seconds, 2 x 30, 2 x 45, 2 x 30, 2 x 15. Felt OK but steep hill / one warm-down.
FRIDAY. Rest.
SATURDAY. Parkrun – felt easy.
SUNDAY. Nine miles – felt very controlled.

And then, all of a sudden, a phone call: "Steve, my knee really hurt on the tempo run today."

I agreed that she should see a physiotherapist as soon as possible. Upon examination, the physio reassured her that the problem was not major, advised her to ease off the running a bit, and gave her exercises to correct the slight imbalance that had caused the pain.

We revised the plan, dialling the long runs down a little, keeping the short hills and efforts, but crucially, after a week off, dividing the tempo runs into shorter segments without compromising on the speed or overall speed-endurance effect.

Those last six weeks before the race were fingers-crossed time, because one is never 100% certain how much an athlete with a slight injury can or should do.

We took it week by week – day by day really.

However, her weekly reports carried encouraging news: "Felt knee slightly, but nothing like before." "Knee felt best it's ever been."

With a taper in the last two weeks, so that she would arrive at the start line with bags of energy and fresh legs, we hit race day.

The plan was to warm up well, and then to try to chip away at the sub-10-minute mile target pace, hopefully giving her a morale boost at each mile.

Her first two miles were slightly over 10 minutes, but she had the confidence to know that it was the crowded field that was slowing her slightly, but that it would soon space out.

Indeed, her third mile was nearer 9:30, and each subsequent split saw her slice significant numbers of seconds from her sub-10 goal. Even a hilly 10th mile was only marginally over 10 minutes, and the last three miles in 9:11, 9:27 and 9:11 proved that her endurance and determination were certainly in place – and that her knee was fine.

It was probably her best-ever run, and a fitting reward for years of running, for months of dedication to this specific race and plan, for her ability to keep the faith when the potentially showstopping knee injury occurred, as well as for the all-important capacity to lay it all on the line on the day.

As Brendan Foster used to say: "It's all very well running 100 miles a week in training, but you still have to screw yourself up in the race."

As I watched this athlete sprint towards the finish line (albeit with something in my eye!), I knew that she had put it all out there, working for every last second that she could possibly take off her previous best.

I hope that you too can find a target that motivates you, that you can devise a plan to get you from here to there, and then that you can follow that plan as faithfully as life will allow, that you can make an effort that is true to your training on race day, and that you will reap the rewards that you deserve for such dedication.

Nothing worth having is ever easy.

"What lap are you on?" he asked.

"Same one as you, mate!" I said.

I have mentioned this race before, but it is one of the best examples I have of the point I am trying to make.

Around 50 miles into the National 100km Championships of 1994, I had just come level with the man in third place. Having held the bronze medal position for more than 10 miles, he looked a bit worried!

On a hot day, the two leaders were miles ahead, but lots of the favourites had dropped out, so, from a position in the twenties early on, I suddenly, amazingly, found myself challenging for the last available medal.

We ran side by side for a few miles before I managed to ease ahead (nothing easy about it, really). The mile-long circuit included a lap of the track and, with about three miles to go, I saw my competitor entering the track as I was leaving it – meaning I had a 400m lead. Surely I couldn't be caught now?

That was when the hamstring cramps struck!

Another lap – still the same lead.

I plugged away and did indeed win the bronze medal. It was a personal best by half an hour and was my first national running medal. It meant I got to stand on the podium. I even got drugs tested!

Seizing that unexpected opportunity – and not giving up under pressure – were certainly worth it that day.

"Are you as proud of yourself as I am of me?" The very perceptive lady with 'ICELAND' on her vest asked me.

We had simultaneously come to the same realisation – that we might actually finish this race!

The Swiss Alpine Marathon, based in Davos, was the largest mountain running festival in the world, and the K78 event (78km) was at the time (2008) the planet's premier mountain ultra-marathon. The last Saturday of our week there saw the staging of a range of races from 10 to 78 kilometres, to suit all abilities.

I am immodestly sharing a story from my running past because I hope it might help you through the tough times.

The 2:09 Events Limited group, of which I was a part, had spent the week acclimatising to the 2,600m altitude, and running and hiking among the beautiful alpine meadows and peaks.

I had spent most of the week worrying about the cut-offs!

An ageing ultra-runner of 50, I was still too proud to enter nothing but the longest event on offer! Not the measly 42km for me, oh no!! And, so, I found myself analysing the strict schedule of times at which each part of the 78km course would close.

The first 30km were mostly downhill to Filisur, with a 3:40 cut-off at that point. I would get a decent chunk up on the schedule during that time, I thought, and have something in hand for the demanding mountain traverses to come!

Little did I know.

We rose before dawn, had breakfast in the hotel and made our way to the stadium. Most of our group were doing one of the two K42s on offer, with only three of us opting to go longer.

The buzz in the stadium was fantastic – all shapes, all sizes, all nationalities, all nervous – and all too soon we were off, looping through the town to a chorus of "Good luck" from the rest of the group who had come out to cheer us on.

Now, those first 30km were indeed mostly downhill, but there were also some long climbs, some technical wooded sections and, crucially, some bottlenecks where the early volume of runners meant frustrating minutes were lost waiting for my turn to go over a stile or pass through a gate.

Filisur approached. OK, I've got a bit of time in hand. Loop through the town. Where's the bloody cut-off point? Another corner. Not much time left now. At last, I reached it in 3:37 – with three minutes to spare.

From here, the course basically climbs for over 10km, meaning I had to walk long stretches and I was convinced I would not reach the next cut-off in time, which made morale a problem. I had till 4:50 to reach Bergün; I was somewhat surprised to get there in 4:44.

Lordy, I had never spent so long in a race, **knowing** – not thinking – that I would not finish.

Chants had a cut-off of 6:05; again, it came slightly earlier than expected in 5:58. (It was here that an English guy in our group got to the cut-off 40 seconds too late and was ordered on to the bus back to Davos! Swiss timing!)

And now the real work began!

From Chants, the course rises very steeply to the start of the Panoramaweg at the ski hut at Keschhütte. I mean **very steeply** – it was agony even walking.

At some point, I turned a corner and I could see the hut far above me – I had till 7:30 to get there. I was walking with a Belgian guy in a distinctive orange jacket. He had finished the K78 for the last eight years; he wanted to make it 10. I looked up at the hut again and apologised – I had to leave him and press on – over the river, round the switchbacks, up, up, up.

7:23!!

It was only now that I allowed myself to think that maybe, just maybe, I could do this.

I looked back down the mountain and saw my orange-clad former companion – I was sorry to know that he was not going to make it nine years in a row.

It's at Keschhütte that the race has a team of doctors who stop each runner as they come through, look into our eyes, and ask us how we feel.

They have absolute power: they pull out those whom they consider to be too spaced out to continue.

This is because, apart from anything else, the next section over the Panoramaweg includes several mini glaciers and many exposed ridges. In other words, you've got to have your wits about you!

I was obviously looking less vacant than usual, because they allowed me to carry on, and I was able to walk and run the next two hours or so, along the well-named Panoramaweg (panorama way), taking in the alpine sights (including the K42 runners who were routed along the valley floor far below our vantage point), watching where I was putting my feet and trying to take it one mile at a time.

It was just after Dürrboden (cut-off 9:50; time 9:37) with just the 'easy' run back down into Davos to come, that my Icelandic friend summed up our achievement.

And so, we jogged through the beautiful alpine meadows, over streams, past farms, to reach the outskirts of Davos, where several of the 2:09 Events Limited crowd had gathered to cheer us in. From there it was a circuitous route around and through the town, finally running along the main drag, high-fiving the beer-quaffing locals who were sitting outside the cafés in the warmth of the evening sun.

Into the stadium, and a finish in 11:25:32 (cut-off 12 hours).

Medal, t-shirt, drinks. (A compatriot made the mistake of drinking a beer just after crossing the line and found that it locked up his jaw so completely that he was unable to speak or eat for the rest of the night!)

I walked back to our hotel and went into the restaurant where the rest were already dining. Much to my surprise, they stood up and burst into applause.

I have been lucky enough to have experienced quite a few moments of intense pride, satisfaction and fulfilment in my running career, but this – coming from my fellow competitors – ranks among the very best.

More than that, finishing was so precious to me because I had achieved what I had at several points convinced myself I could not. Against all the odds, I had kept the belief.

CHAPTER 23

SIMPLE – WHAT'S THE SECRET TO A HEALTHY LIFE?

"What will survive of us is love."

AFTER I HAD finished speaking at the club get-together, a lady approached me and said: "Steve, I try to be healthy and follow the professional advice on exercise and diet and all that, but it's all so complicated, and some of it, to be frank, is contradictory. What should I focus on?"

Great question, I thought, but actually being healthy should be **SIMPLE**.

(Now, I am not preaching here, or telling you what to do; these are just some of my ideas.)

SLEEP SEVEN, SOUNDLY. Without sleep, you can't operate for long. "Sleep that knits up the raveled sleave of care / The death of each day's life, sore labor's bath / Balm of hurt minds, great nature's second course / Chief nourisher in life's feast," said William Shakespeare's *Macbeth*. Whilst 'a solid eight hours' has been the prescribed nocturnal dose for a while, science now agrees that seven hours is enough, as long as it is restful. And we all know that not eating close to bedtime, nor watching screens of any kind late at night, having the room at the right temperature, with fresh air, can all help. I would also say, try to let life's worries go. Write down a list of anything that is on your mind, anything that you must remember to do the next day. I believe that, by setting those aside in that way, you are more likely to achieve the peace of mind that will encourage lasting, restful sleep.

INVEST INTERNALLY, INTELLIGENTLY. 'You are what you eat' is a mantra we have all heard. And we are quite literally what we eat and drink, as our muscles' and bodily systems' recovery – as well as our cell regeneration – can only utilise the chemicals that we provide. You will be all too aware of the so-called unhealthy foods, good foods and superfoods, but science has moved on from the time in the last century when fat was the bad guy. Most studies now agree that sugar is the real culprit, and that high fructose corn syrup (HFCS) is particularly bad for us. Without getting too bogged down in the science bit, HFCS does not stimulate insulin, which attempts to balance the body's sugar levels, in the same way that other types of sugar do. Instead, it goes straight to the liver to trigger the production of fat. And, of course, HFCS is in everything that we like – fizzy drinks, fast food, sweets, and even bread, cereals and baked beans – as well as being behind the fortunes of many household brand names!

MOVE MORE MILES. "One is always nearer by not keeping still," said the English poet, Thom Gunn (1929–2004). I had this quote on my wall at college, and my roommate amended part of it to, "by not keeping S.Till". Anyway, in this (for many) sedentary life of sitting in front of a computer, behind

a desk, a check-out or counter, of driving even the shortest distances, of taking the lift instead of the stairs, our muscles weaken and our vital cardiovascular system degenerates over time. The recent craze for taking 10,000 steps a day is a great antidote to that. However, allow me to testify from personal experience that even a tiny bit of more intense movement can work wonders. I can walk for many hours or I can run for 20 minutes – I know which one burns more calories, and for longer!

PUSH, PULL, PRESS. Alongside the cardiovascular activity, experts consider some sort of weight-training to be equally vital. Now it doesn't have to be in a gym, and it won't make you look like Arnie, but a couple of sessions a week can transform you. This is because muscle strength is what we lose most of, fastest, as we age. And maintaining muscle mass, and even increasing it, means our body will burn more calories in everything that we do. So, press-ups – on your toes, on your knees or against the wall or a table – sit-ups of any sort, walking briskly up flights of stairs, or simply getting up from a chair repeatedly, are all great. Hold a heavy bag in each hand by your sides, bend your arms to bring them to shoulder height, and then press them over your head. (The suggested bag used to be of sugar, but, of course, you wouldn't have that in the house now, would you?!) And, once you've outgrown your domestic gym, consider joining a public one. They really aren't intimidating anymore. For obvious commercial reasons, they go out of their way to welcome everyone and to make themselves a safe and comfortable environment for people of all ages, shapes and sizes.

LIVE, LEAVE LIGHTLY. "I have spread my dreams under your feet. Tread softly because you tread on my dreams." So wrote Irish poet, W.B. Yeats (1865–1939). This one is as much for our planet as our bodies. If we can drive less and walk, run or cycle more, and when we walk, take only pictures and leave only footprints (probably a Native American saying); if we can live and eat as sustainably as we can; if we can buy and consume what is grown or reared or produced locally; if we can volunteer or donate when we are able; then we are leaving behind us a world that is more vital, more vibrant and, most importantly, more viable for our children.

EMBRACE, ENJOY EMPATHY. "No man is an island," wrote English poet and Dean of St Paul's Cathedral, John Donne (1572–1631). "And therefore never send to know for whom the bell tolls; it tolls for thee." We are social animals – or most of us are, the exception being runners who are injured or have had a bad race – and we are meant to interact, to communicate, and to nourish each other. The Covid-19 pandemic, in snatching away so much of that interaction, actually taught us to value it more. The simple pleasures that we all took for granted – the chat with a neighbour, coffee with friends, a pint in the pub, walking together, playing sport, sharing culture, even a smile or a kind word between strangers on the street – now seem to have more meaning and greater resonance. Philip Larkin (1922–1985) wrote: "What will survive of us is love." And in love's broadest sense – the positive, empathetic feelings we hold for any other person and the incalculable impact we have on our fellow humans every day – that is surely true.

CHAPTER 24

SECRET – WHAT'S THE SECRET?

"The secret of distance running is about to unfold."

Mo Farah

SO INTONED BBC commentator Brendan Foster as Mo Farah hit the front in the Olympic 5,000m final at the London 2012 Games. The secret there was to take the lead with about two laps to go – and stay there! Easier said than done, though easier for Farah from the front, than for his rivals trying to make up a yard or two when Mo's doing a 53-second last lap.

The secrets of running for you and me may be a little more basic than that, but no less crucial for our lasting running contentment.

Over the years, I have run many miles and coached many runners, and I have seen myself and others make some silly mistakes and forget some obvious 'rules'.

Here are my running secrets.

- Cut your toenails.
- Make sure you're hydrated before a run.
- Buy decent running shoes.
- Flat routes are easier than hilly ones, though slightly undulating ones, where you have a bit of downhill relief from time to time, may be easier than both.
- Ease into your run – walk a bit first.
- Keep a log – it really helps your motivation if you can see how far you've come.
- Establish a routine and try and do a bit more – a bit further or a bit faster – every fortnight or so.
- Find a friend to jog with – you are far more likely to get out there if you know you'll be letting someone down if you don't.
- Have a target – this is the BIG secret! Having a target is the 'rule' of running that I bang on about the most – apart from the one about not running with scissors in your hand, of course. Your target could be running all the way up that hill, or running three miles without stopping, or running every day in February. I think that something more public is going to be more motivating for you.
- A parkrun or a race may be scary, but if you register for parkrun or enter a race, and tell your family and friends about it, then you'll probably do it!
- There are parkruns all over the area – just go to the parkrun UK website and you'll soon find a map under 'events' – 'parkrun events' that shows parkrun symbols practically covering the entire country. You register once on the site, print off your barcode and you can do any parkrun – anywhere in the world – free of charge!

You can run, jog, walk, walk your dog (in most events) or push your pushchair. You can hula hoop your way round if you really want to! There is always a first timers' briefing, so that you know exactly what to expect and how it all works. And you won't be last – there are Tail Walkers at the back to make sure everyone goes the right way, and to chat to and encourage everyone.

- Then there are races. These are not the scary monsters that you may think. They are friendly, inclusive and most of them cater for all abilities. Marshals will look after your baggage, there's a water station, and there are refreshments and toilets onsite. That is the case for many local races. You only have to do a quick search online to find events near you. And there are loads – on-road, off-road, flat, hilly, short, long, round towns or through countryside – there is something for everyone.

For those who may be put off by the thought of a race, and the thought of being in the same competition as elite athletes, and feeling a bit out of place, I offer this story:

I remember when I was a fledgling race walker back in the 1970s. I'd finished down the field in a 10km race in Essex. I happened to be leaving the changing room to walk round to the post-race refreshments in the church hall, at the same time as Roger Mills, who's from Ilford.

Now, Roger was European bronze medallist in the 20km walk in 1974, and he had just won the race.

I had seen him break the world mile-walk record (6:08.9) at Crystal Palace that year. I had even asked for his autograph afterwards. He was my hero. I didn't dare talk to him. But he turned to me.

"You know, Steve, I've been looking forward to this cup of tea for the last four miles," he said. And at that moment I realised he was human, like me.

Maybe that's the biggest secret of all. They are all human. Paula Radcliffe came 299th in her first cross-country race, but she worked hard and improved.

That's the great thing about running – and exercise in general. With a bit of hard work and a lot of patience, you can achieve something you thought you couldn't.

Someone human like you and me can appear superhuman – or, at the very least, we can surprise a few people (those disbelieving relatives) along the way!

That's the real secret – but, ssh, don't tell anyone.

CHAPTER 25
START – WHAT AM I WAITING FOR?

"The longest journey starts with a single step."

Pen Hadow, Arctic explorer

IS THIS THE most depressing proverb in history? For some, though, taking that single step is the biggest challenge.

"I could be loaded into an ambulance, smiling."[17]

Matthew Pinsent, four-time Olympic rowing champion, seemed like a pretty tough sort of guy. But, he admitted in his book, *A Lifetime in a Race*, that his fear of the pain of competition was so great that he wished that the minibus that was taking him and the rest of the team to the final of the coxless fours could be involved in an accident. He said he would have been put in the ambulance, "smiling", having been relieved of the agony of the test.

Chris Hoy, six-time Olympic cycling champion and as level-headed a bloke as you are likely to meet, talks of sitting in the middle of the velodrome, especially before his kilo time trial finals, wishing he could be anywhere else but there.

"I can't do it. I've lost too much training. I'll do 50km instead of 50 miles."

You will remember Lisa, the lady who desperately wanted to mark her 50th birthday with a memorable run. The story is relevant to reprise here.

We sat down and chatted about it, and we came up with the idea of her running 50 miles. I suggested that doing it all in one go was asking a lot, so why not do it over a weekend – with the majority of the mileage being covered on the Saturday, with the triumphant remainder on the Sunday?

She agreed – and we sorted out an interesting course, a convenient date and a training plan.

Life got in the way. Injuries and other commitments intervened to make Lisa's build-up less than perfect, and two weeks before the scheduled

---

17 *A Lifetime in a Race*, Matthew Pinsent, page 319.

ultra-run, she emailed me to say that she had lost so much training (and confidence) and that she was going to do 50km instead.

I thought about it for a while and then replied: "You can do 50km if you like but you will regret it afterwards. This is not about it being manageable or easy to do, or anything like that – it is because it is difficult to do, that you are doing it, and why we run marathons and test ourselves. I repeat, it is precisely because it is difficult that you are doing it, and why you wanted to run 50 miles in the first place."

And then the clincher: "And, anyway, I will shout at you if you don't do it." (I know my athletes!)

The lady in question said that, once she had received that email, she simply decided that she could do it – and did it.

"I really don't think I'll do it on Sunday. There's too much else going on."

The next example concerns another of my athletes, Yvonne, who had been extremely diligent in her training for an ambitious new half marathon personal best of under two hours. But she had also started a demanding job, in a new city, and, on top of that, also needed to pass exams to maintain her career's skyrocketing trajectory.

The Thursday before the race, she rang me and expressed her fears.

We talked through her training, what I thought she was capable of, and the process she needed to follow to get to the start line in the best possible shape three days later.

I also sent her an email: "Remember, whatever you do on Sunday or don't do, what you are asking of yourself is very difficult. To parcel up all of that training and determination, and deploy it perfectly over two hours, that's hard. World-class hard. I know that, before all of my PB attempts, I just wanted to crawl away and hide. But you try and get into the process – get up, eat, go to the loo, drink, get there, loo, warm-up, drink, start – and in this way, try and creep up on the monster that you are fighting. I am not ignoring all of the other stuff swirling round your head – I know it's hugely difficult to put all that to one side and commit to a 100% effort when thoughts are nagging away at you – but believe in your training, stick to the process, and who knows?"

That Sunday, watching her sprinting towards a finish clock that showed 1:58, knowing what she had been through, I must have had something in my eye!

The idea of creeping up on the monster you are fighting is a fertile one, I think. I am not one for eating the frog first thing. In his book, *Eat That Frog*, Brian Tracy says you should identify your most difficult task of the day and do it before anything else.

But running a great race – or writing a book – is difficult and you have to be right in the zone. Tracy's idea seems to me to be a recipe for a compromised attempt at your most important goal. It's like trying to run a personal best without warming up.

But how on earth do you get into that zone?

I think, as I say, you creep up on it.

A bit like the 'get up, eat, go to the loo, drink, get there, loo, warm-up, drink, start' process that I reminded Yvonne about. There are ways of doing this in all walks of life.

Writers in particular go on about the tricks they use to start writing each day. I have heard even the greatest writers say that sometimes they just beg their god to be allowed to write the worst sentence in the world – and hopefully go on from there.

I know from my own experience that facing a blank sheet of paper – or an empty screen – is pretty intimidating. If I am stuck, then I admit that I will resort to simply typing my name and the date at the top, perhaps adding a provisional title and draft number.

Then I might jot down any notes I've made about the piece, maybe working one or two of these up into reasonable sentences along the way, and, before I know it, I am at least a little way towards starting to write.

And, most importantly, that blank screen has lost its terror for me!

There are countless tales of sportspeople, athletes, runners, getting terrified before their greatest challenges. The greater the challenge, the greater the terror – but the bigger the sense of satisfaction, if you do indeed feel the fear but do it anyway.

Some would say that, if your goal's not intimidating, it's not big enough.

And it's not just **before** the event that you can sabotage yourself.

In 1972, Dave Wottle had qualified for the US Olympic team in both 800m and 1,500m, even equalling the world record in the shorter event, but not many people gave him much of a hope in the Games themselves.

His knees were bad, restricting his training; he had married his wife, Jan, in July and was using the trip to Munich in September as part of their honeymoon (eliciting all-too-predictable comments from the press); and the overwhelming favourite for the 800m was Yevgeni Arzhanov from the USSR.

Arzhanov had won the 1971 European Championships, the US–USSR meeting and the European Indoor Championships. He was said to be able to run 10.4 for 100m, and he trained along Lydiard principles (Arthur Lydiard was a New Zealand coach who advocated all runners clocking 100 miles a week in the build-up period) – a dynamic combination of speed and endurance.

For some context, Arzhanov is Ukrainian and is currently struggling to know where to live during the Russian onslaught.

Watch the YouTube video of the 1972 final – it is a masterclass in pacing and not panicking.

See Wottle start so far back that he is almost out of shot after just 200m. Watch him gradually make up ground towards the bell and just after.

And, with 300m to go, see Arzhanov (red vest) panic and move from sixth to first in about 50 yards.

Wottle comes through behind him, and eventually, amazingly triumphs. But this would not have been possible had he not got his pace exactly right and precisely even – every 200m being run in 26 point-something seconds – and had Arzhanov not panicked, put himself in lactate debt and have his legs turn to jelly with about 30m to go.

A bit closer to home, I will recap the story of my being in contention for the bronze medal at the National 100km Championships in Greenwich Park in 1994. The first two runners were well ahead, but many of the other main contenders had dropped out, leaving me in with a chance of a podium place.

The trouble was, with about 10 miles to go, I had two other runners for company.

On each lap, we looped round the running track, and I managed to squeeze out a lead on one of the others, leaving the track as he entered, meaning I had about 400m on him. Fingers crossed, that should do.

But the other runner was dangerous.

However, to my astonishment, with about five miles left, he went off for a massage! Now a massage would certainly relieve his sore legs, but the time lost would definitely kill off any chance he had of a medal. Clearly, he could not face the suffering in the battle out there on the course.

His head, as they say, had gone.

And then there's another story from the same year, which starts with a voice ringing out across the Humberside athletics track.

"Come on, Steve, you can do this."

It was my wife, Beverley. There were 30 minutes left in my 24-hour race and, reduced to a slow walk, I knew I was going to miss my personal best by about a mile – and with it, the chance to really catch the eye of the Great Britain ultra-distance selectors. With 130-odd miles in my legs, I had every excuse to be tired – and to be intimidated by the remaining half hour.

But a greater prize was at stake (the possibility of that GB vest), and I don't really know what happened next, but I suddenly started running eight-minute miles, managing somehow to keep that going until the bitter end, so that I actually beat my PB by a mile, won the race, and did indeed attract interest from the powers that be.

But few have as much reason to be intimidated by a challenge as Pen Hadow, when he lay in a bare concrete bunker, having just been dropped on the Canadian edge of the North Polar ice cap, at the start of his 2003 attempt to be the first person to walk solo and unsupported from the Canadian side to the Pole – crucially, against the polar drift. The attempt was a promise to his father.

But lying there, he had to listen to the extreme blizzard outside. He knew that his sled was currently at its heaviest (265lbs, because being unsupported meant carrying all his food from day one) and he'd hardly be able to pull it at first. He also knew that he'd have to swim at times, in an immersion suit, across gaps in the ice, just hoping there wasn't a polar bear around. He also knew that, walking against the flow, he'd barely make any real progress each day. Naturally, he wondered whether he could do it.

Well, he did make it – in 64 days. He is still the only person ever to have done it, and he is likely to remain in that way unique, because of the melting of the polar ice.

So, the next time you're intimidated by a challenge, ask yourself if you have as much right to be intimidated as Pen did.

And the next time you're **not** intimidated by a challenge, ask yourself if it's big enough!

I'm not asking you to outswim polar bears or win Olympic finals, well, not until we have got to know each other a little better. I am saying, why not set yourself a challenge?

It could be running. It might well be in another sport. It could dwell in a different walk of life entirely.

But what is that overriding challenge for you? What is the goal that is borne out of your passion for something, that is going to excite you until its fulfilment and beyond? What is the objective that sings to your very soul?

What is the challenge that is, literally or metaphorically, going to get you out on that practice track on a cold winter's morning?

Set yourself the right goal – its rectitude is vital and is the entire foundation for your success. If it's not right, it can't give you the necessary motivation (see the first three chapters).

And then do it (see chapter four)!

There are going to be days when the task you've set yourself, to get you to where you want to be, is worse than eating a frog. But you know you should do it. You know deep down you want to do it. Because you know all too well what it will give you if you do.

The achievement. The satisfaction. The happiness. The enjoyment.

All I would say is, just start. Just literally or metaphorically, get your kit on, have that last glass of water, check your technology if you must, step out of the door, and start.

Just start.

Or, as someone once said, "Get on with it!"

BEGINNERS' SECTION

THE FIRST, EXCITING STEPS

YOU WILL IMPROVE, change, go further, go faster, run easier, and even eventually enjoy it. I promise you – or your money back!

This section is dedicated to anyone who doesn't currently run but thinks they might like to start. Someone once said that all of us are athletes – it's just that some of us are in training, and some not.

But starting running is exciting. You're embarking on an adventure. Almost everyone who starts running, will indeed improve. It's a given. So, watching things change over the first weeks and months – even years – is exciting and inspiring. Your body will change shape. Your experience of each run will develop over time. And, of course, how fast you run, how far you can run, and how you feel when running – all of these markers will be transformed out of all recognition.

So, in this section, I cover how to start, what to expect, how to progress, as well as how parkrun may be able to help you. I offer you a sample schedule. I suggest the reasons why you might run and why running is simply the best exercise going.

I answer the perennial runner's question – how fast should I expect to progress?

And I give you some ideas about common running issues or problems, like how to establish a favourite running loop, how to run first thing in the morning, dealing with injuries, and running in the autumn and winter.

Finally – as you get further into your running – I discuss things like how those dreaded hills might be a friend in disguise, how to find the right coach, and what to consider when entering your first race.

I hope it will be useful and launch you on what should be an exciting journey of discovery.

Good luck!

YOU WANT TO START RUNNING – BUT HOW?

HERE ARE 10 tips to get you moving.

GET MEDICAL CLEARANCE. If you haven't done any exercise for a while, or you just want peace of mind, it's always wise to see your GP and make sure that they can give you the all-clear to start.

CUT YOUR TOENAILS. Jogging will make your toes hit the end of your shoes more forcefully than when you're walking, so it's best if your toenails are quite short.

SHOES. Running, or jogging, is not an expensive hobby, so it is important to invest in a good pair of trainers. These should be comfortable, fit correctly, and should respond to any idiosyncrasies that your feet may display (basically, do they turn in or turn out?). There are many specialist running shops now, where they can put you on a treadmill, analyse your gait and recommend the best shoes for your stride, build and intended surfaces.

EAT A LIGHT MEAL ONE OR TWO HOURS BEFORE YOU RUN. Everyone is different. You may find you need more or less time than this, or that you can tolerate a heavier meal. Experiment and see what will fuel you for the exercise, without making you feel bloated when you do it.

DRINK WATER. Make sure you are hydrated before you start, and remember to rehydrate afterwards, even in winter, and even when you think you haven't perspired (you have!). Water is better than coffee, tea, beer, wine or gin. Sorry!

FIND A FLAT ROUTE. Starting to run can be hard, so you don't need the extra stress of a hill to run up. Certainly, for your first few outings – and your first few hundred yards – find a route that is flat or even slightly downhill (at least to start with). You may find that you prefer pavement, or the park, or the woods. Find a route that you enjoy, whilst being aware of the obvious safety aspects.

WALK BEFORE YOU CAN RUN. Start by walking for a few minutes. This will gently warm your muscles and get you ready to take your first running steps in a more prepared state.

RUN. Just start jogging. The speed does not matter. You can try and jog for so many seconds, for so many steps, between lampposts, to the next corner, or whatever your Garmin® or Fitbit® says. Choose what works for you, but try and keep to a schedule. What I mean by this is if you find you can run for 30 seconds (say), try and do that, then walk for 30 or 60 seconds, or whatever you need to recover, and then repeat the run/walk sequence a few times. You will be surprised how far you can get.

TRY AND BE REGULAR AND PROGRESSIVE. Try and go out at least three times a week – not on consecutive days – and, once you are getting more comfortable with the runs, see if you can run for longer (45 rather than 30 seconds; six run/walk sequences rather than three). Keep a log – you are more likely to keep at it, if you can see how far you've come already.

BE PROUD OF EACH STEP YOU ARE TAKING. Believe me, unless you are Mo Farah, there will always be someone better at running than you – and, I guarantee, there will always be someone worse. Well done for taking those steps. Especially that first one!

You've started to walk/jog/run – but now what?

SO, YOU'VE STARTED – well done – you've done the hardest bit!

By now, you'll know how good it feels to get moving, to cover a few minutes, even a couple of miles, under your own steam. You'll hopefully have felt the physical and emotional 'glow' or 'high' you get afterwards.

You'll also realise that it can be hard. Getting out of the door can be hard. Taking the first jogging or running steps can be hard. That hill's hard!

But it's worth it. **You're** worth it. Your health, your well-being, your happiness are worth it.

So how do you make sure you keep going?

Here are some tips:

ESTABLISH A ROUTINE.

Plan three or four times a week when you can exercise, and try and space them out over the days. An example could be a long walk on a Sunday, a short jog on Tuesday and Thursday, and some other exercise on a Saturday.

KNOW YOUR NEEDS.

After a few outings, you will get to know your 'jogging self' a bit better. What do I mean by that? You will know it's best to go out in the mornings – or the evenings. You will know that you need at least an hour between eating or drinking and jogging. You will know that you need a glass of water just before you go out. You will know that you hate that hill and you need to go the other way round the block.

MAKE IT PROGRESSIVE. Assuming that you will jog/run two or three times a week (from time to time try and do a bit more), not every time you go out, not even every week, try and move it up a gear every couple of weeks. Here's an example: Let's say you can jog for three minutes and then walk for two minutes, four times in a session. Try and jog a little longer, walk a little less or do it five or six times rather than three or four. And you know what? At some point, you will magically find yourself going further than you thought you could!

FIND A FRIEND. Exercise is much more pleasant in company, so if you've got a friend, relation or colleague who is pursuing the same sort of goal, and you are roughly the same standard, then arrange to meet once or more a week to jog/run together. You are more likely to do it if you have agreed to meet ('Don't want to let Sue down') and the session itself will pass more quickly and sociably.

KEEP A LOG. Record what you do, even if you haven't done very much, or it's less than you planned. Just knowing you're going to write it down may encourage you to do more. (Just as having a coach or personal trainer and knowing you've got to report back to them every week will also make you more inclined to do more.) Even after a couple of weeks, just looking at what you've done – say, six jogs in 14 days – should inspire you to keep at it. "I mustn't just stop now and let all of that be in vain." Or, "I've done the hardest bit – Steve said so!" Just jot down as much or as little as you like – 'Jogged with Ben – walked five minutes, then jogged 2 / walked 2 x 5 – bit windy, and hill was hard'.

HAVE A TARGET. It's always easier to hit a target if you've got one! Yes, do focus on week-by-week or fortnight-by-fortnight progress, as I say, but why not have a longer-term aim in mind? What inspires you? Everyone's different. What do you want to achieve? Maybe it's to do a 5km without walking, to do the Wednesday loop without walking, to run a 10km one day, to run a mile in under 12 minutes, or to be able to jog while your children cycle. What target makes you think, 'Wow – that would be great if I could do that'? It may be too early for you to have a target just yet, and it could well change over time anyway. I am not saying you've got to aim big, but it's something to bear in mind. And it is something that could provide that important spur in the weeks and months to come.

Just keep going.

Pain is temporary, pride is forever.

Good luck!

What is parkrun all about?

IF YOU WANT to move more, to start jogging and to perhaps run a bit, parkrun could well be all about **you**!

Every Saturday morning, about 200,000 people of all shapes, sizes and ambitions meet in open spaces around the UK – as well as across the globe – to walk, jog, run, push buggies, walk their dogs, or volunteer over a measured, marshalled 5km route.

I am not an official parkrun spokesperson, so this is just what I have experienced.

There are many wonderful things about parkrun. Perhaps the two most wonderful are that it is free (register once online at www.parkrun.org.uk and you can do any parkrun anywhere in the world) and that it is inclusive.

What do I mean by that?

Hen parties have hula hooped the entire 5km!

It is for everyone. The atmosphere at parkruns is extremely welcoming. There is always a first timers' briefing, so that everyone knows what to expect. There are always Tail Walkers, who walk at the back of the field, so that no one (no visitor, no first-timer) is last. It is a run, not a race. People chat to you (if you are open to it) beforehand and stay on for coffee afterwards.

I have seen squaddies run it in army boots with a full pack. I have seen hen parties hula hoop round the entire 5km!

And parkrun may just be what **you** have been looking for, to help you attain your fitness goals. I will explain how, but first, let me give you two examples of how parkrun has helped other people.

Debs (not her real name) lost her husband when they were both in their forties, and understandably really struggled with depression. She could hardly bring herself to go out, and comfort eating meant that she put on more and more weight.

Like with Kathy in Chapter 18, a friend told Debs about parkrun, but she thought it was for fast, slim runners. Her friend persisted and persuaded Debs to just go along.

What she found was a supportive community of smiling faces. She managed one lap of the three-lap course that day and felt "more alive". A seed had been sown, and she returned the next week.

She started going for walks during the week and eating a bit more healthily. She started losing weight, instead of putting it on, and, of course, the weekly date with parkrun kept her motivated.

After several weeks, she completed the whole 5km course. She was astounded to find lots of people waiting for her, cheering madly.

That was a couple of years – and a lifetime – ago now, and since then she has done things like join a local running club and run a half marathon.

Steve (his real name) was a good class runner in his early years, running sub-three-hour marathons, winning the odd medal and even representing Great Britain. But in his fifties, he lost motivation. He knew he'd never set another personal best, so what was the point?

COMMUNITY, CHAT, COFFEE, CAKE, CAMARADERIE AND CHEERING!

Like Debs, but for different reasons, he put on weight, and didn't run very much at all. And, of course, as he ran less, he weighed more.

Then along came parkrun.

Suddenly, I had a target every Saturday morning. I could use it as a training run, or even a jog with some friends. Or I could make an effort and try for a personal best. With so many different events around, if I got stuck chasing a time at one event, I could move on to another, flatter or hillier, parkrun and try and get a personal best there.

I started to run more during the week and eat better, too. I eventually lost four stone.

parkrun is now an important part of my week. It came along at just the right time in my fitness life.

But it is more than that. It is a community, it is chat, it is coffee and cake, it is camaraderie, it is cheering.

And parkrun may be able to help **you** to attain your fitness goals. It could slot into your week (it's 9am every Saturday) and help you run further or faster than before. It could give your week a structure – 'jog with Sue on Tuesday morning; jog on my own Thursday night; parkrun Saturday; long walk Sunday' – and a momentum – 'must run today or I'll feel it on Saturday'.

In 2022, parkrun launched its parkwalk initiative to show to the world that people could move around that 5km in any way they choose. They wanted to remove the trepidation that some folk might have about anything with 'run' in its name. And I know that, at my home parkrun, many have come along just because of that change.

That's what parkrun is all about. It is many things to many people – a competitive run, a 5km chat, a training session, time with my kids, time with my dog, literally a walk in the park or the woods, what I do to deserve cake. And parkrun could just be all about you.

Why not give it a try?

WHAT WOULD BE A SAMPLE SCHEDULE?

AFTER THE INITIAL weeks of simply getting used to jogging, perhaps you could consider a more structured approach?

Walk for five minutes, jog for one minute, walk for one minute, jog for one minute, walk for one minute, jog for one minute, and walk for another five minutes.

How did that feel?

If it's hard, three days later, walk for five minutes, jog for 30 seconds, walk for one minute, jog for 30 seconds, walk for one minute, jog for 30 seconds, and walk for five minutes. Repeat this every three days until it gets easier, then try to jog for one minute, walk for one minute, jog for one minute, walk for one minute, and jog for one minute.

If it's easy, two days later, walk for five minutes, jog for as long as you can until it gets uncomfortable (either your legs get heavy or your breathing becomes laboured), walk for the same time you jogged for, repeat the jog and try and go for as long as you did before, walk for the same time again, jog for the same time again, and walk for five minutes.

I'm assuming you've taken notes (!!) from the first few parts of this Beginners' Section, and got your GP's clearance if necessary, cut your toenails, got a decent pair of jogging shoes, eaten and drunk water a little time before, and found a flat-ish route.

From here on, there are as many schedules as there are people. And there are at least three things you can vary – the **3Rs**.

No, not Reading, wRiting and aRithmetic – though maths does come into it!

RUN-TIME, RECOVERY AND REPETITIONS

You can run (jog) for longer. You can take a shorter recovery. You can repeat the cycle more times.

So, someone who started out doing the above – walk for five minutes, jog for one minute, walk for one minute, jog for one minute, walk for one minute, jog for one minute, walk for five minutes – after eight weeks, might walk for five minutes, jog for four minutes, walk for two minutes, jog for four minutes, walk for two minutes, jog for four minutes, walk for two minutes, jog for four minutes, walk for two minutes, jog for four minutes, and walk for five minutes.

This might more easily be stated as 5w, 4j/2w x 5, 3w.

But everyone is different. You are an experiment of one. The important thing is to put in a little bit of effort every time you go out, not to get hung up on what anybody else is doing, and to look for progression.

I am not talking about doing more every session, not even every week, but gradually over time, your wonderful human body will adapt to what you are asking it to do – and you will be able to do more, to need less recovery, and to repeat it more often.

Keep a note of what you do, and you will be surprised how far you can go – literally as well as figuratively. An exercise log will remind you what you've done and will motivate you to keep it up.

My number one tip? Even if you don't feel like it, just put on your gear and get out of the door. Promise yourself you'll walk for 10 minutes. It'll often turn into a jog, or a longer walk.

As someone once said, 'just do it'!

Why do you run? There are as many different reasons as there are runners

BY NOW, I hope you are into a schedule of regular running, but…have you ever stopped and thought about why you really do it? Here are a few of **my** reasons.

TO GET FIT OR TO KEEP FIT. We all know that jogging/running is one of the easiest, most convenient ways of achieving this – no complicated equipment, no gym to get to, no court to book, no team to coordinate with. Just put on those shoes and get out of the door!

TO STAVE OFF AGE. All runners look 10 years younger – it's a fact!

TO PLAY LIKE A CHILD. There is a sense that we have lost the ability to play, and that running puts us back into something like the zone our childhood fun represented.

TO EXPERIENCE THE ELEMENTS. There is nothing like being out running to make you appreciate first-hand the vagaries of the British weather. But while you're jogging along, you're keeping warm; and once you've gone a few minutes, you don't mind the rain. In fact, you're much better off than the drivers, cyclists and pedestrians struggling through the same conditions. Smile at them! If you want, be smug!

TO PREPARE FOR COMPETITION. Again, only if you want to.

TO BE ABLE TO EAT AND DRINK. Not quite eat and drink anything you like, but certainly a good session makes your internal fire burn more brightly to use up more of those calories.

TO SHARE EXPERIENCES WITH FRIENDS. Like soldiers in battle or climbers on a mountain – though at a lower, less dangerous level – sharing effort, pain even, with friends, makes the bonds between you much stronger.

TO TRAVEL UNDER YOUR OWN STEAM. There is something very satisfying about being able to move across the countryside without transportation, experiencing the land entirely dependent on your own fitness, energy and navigation – just as our ancestors must have done for centuries.

TO EXPLORE. Once you can cover a few miles, you can start to explore. 'I wonder where that footpath goes?' 'Where does that alley come out?' And you can follow it if you have time. Or you can look at your phone, or go home and look at the map, and find out. 'Ah, that's where it goes!'

TO UNWIND. No one ever said: 'I wish I hadn't done that run.' No matter what sort of day you have had, or what sort of challenges you face, a run can help you cope, can put problems into perspective, and generally lift your mood.

TO EXERCISE MY DOG. Though not as much as she'd like!

TO KEEP UP WITH MY CHILDREN. Well, to keep them in sight for a bit.

TO IMPROVE AND TO FEEL THAT IMPROVEMENT. There's nothing like a bit of progress to make you want more – and to be motivated to work for it.

TO FEEL FREE. Maybe leave that phone at home once in a while!

TO REDUCE LIFE TO ITS BASICS OF HEAT, COLD, FOOD, DRINK, ENERGY, FATIGUE, TIME AND DISTANCE. In the 21st century in England, most of us are lucky enough to spend most of our time insulated from the more hostile aspects of the natural world, as well as from thirst, hunger, discomfort and pain. Running reconnects us with a lot of what we have lost.

TO AMAZE A FEW PEOPLE ALONG THE WAY. Running is an amazing sport – and humans are amazing animals. Give yourself enough time – and put in enough effort – and you can transform what you can do. You can run non-stop for 10 minutes. For 30 minutes. All the way up that hill. Complete that first 10km. That first marathon. The distance that took you 45 minutes in week six, now takes 28 minutes. Those close to you will see what you're doing – and they'll see you improve bit by bit. But keep at it, and once in a while, you will amaze them.

Running is simply the best exercise

"YOU CAN'T MOVE for blooming joggers."

Yes, when lockdown began, and the gyms closed, and we were initially limited to an hour outside a day, it seemed that the world suddenly discovered the joy of running. But that's just something that you and I have known all along, isn't it?

I love running. For so many reasons. One of the main ones is that it gives you back as much as you put in. I know that, even if I were coached by Roger Federer, I'd never be any good at tennis, but I can run, and I can improve at running. I may be biased, of course, but I think running is by far the best exercise. Here are 10 good reasons why.

HERE, THERE AND EVERYWHERE. It is so convenient. You don't need much equipment. You don't need a partner to play with or against. You don't need a pool, a court or a pitch. You can do it almost anywhere and at any time. This is proven by the fact that, in order to keep a running streak going, some obsessives have run round airport lounges or the decks of ships! Some people get up outrageously early in the morning to fit it in, or go out late at night. But you shouldn't have to be that extreme. Just keep in mind that running is always available to you.

CAN'T BUY ME LOVE. It is cheap. Do invest in a decent pair of running shoes, because they will do a lot to keep you from getting injured, but, beyond that, you really don't need anything that you don't already own. Of course, once you get hooked, you'll want the latest compression shorts, Garmin®, wireless buds and Nike Vaporflys (other fast running shoes are not available), but for now, the shoes, that old t-shirt and shorts or bottoms will do nicely.

YOU CAN DO IT IF YOU REALLY WANT. Anyone can do it. OK, almost anyone. You should ask your doctor if it is OK to start running, if you are in any doubt. But you can do it – bad knees, bad hips, bad feet – I don't care – you can do it. You may be wise to start with walking, and then power walking (fast walking), and that itself will do you the world of good, but you'll get even more benefit if you can raise that to a jog after a while.

OOH-AAH...JUST A LITTLE BIT. You don't have to do that much. Once you have got into it, just 20–30 minutes of a reasonable effort (so that you sweat and get out of breath) three times a week, is perfectly sufficient to transform your fitness level, burn lots of calories, and get you on to the next stage – you know, the one where you actually enjoy the running!

COME ON, BABY, LIGHT MY FIRE. And that brings me on to the next point – running burns more calories and keeps that metabolic rate stoked for longer. There have been lots of surveys done that conclude this, but I know from my own experience. I can go to the gym and make an intense effort for over an hour – or I can jog for 20 minutes. I know which one will burn more calories for me – and keep burning them for longer – and it's not the gym!

SPICE UP YOUR LIFE. It is endlessly varied. You can run on pavements or roads. You can run on trails or hills. You can run small laps or one big one. You can run point-to-point. You can run round a track. You can stick to short distances. You can go long. You can do sprints or speedwork. You can blast hills. You can run alone. You can run with a friend. You can join a jogging group. You can join a serious running club. You can enter races, or you can simply run for fitness or fun.

ONE, TWO, THREE – THAT'S HOW ELEMENTARY. Running is measurable, endlessly so. If you want to, if this is what motivates you, you can collect an almost infinite amount of data about your running – distances and times obviously, but also steps taken, calories burned, and altitude ascended and descended. Perhaps more importantly, you can analyse your mile or kilometre splits, to see where it all went so right or so wrong.

ALL BY MYSELF. It's just down to you. There's no team to make up for your mistakes – or to share the credit with when you score the winner. It's just you – you stand and fall by your own efforts. Running is, in that respect, a meritocracy, and, let's face it, in this often seemingly grossly unfair world, how many things can you truly say that about? Having said that, if you do end up joining a club, it is great to share your experiences with your colleagues after a race – "ooh, what about that hill at three miles?" "How did you get across that stream?"

THE ONLY WAY IS UP. You get better. I have no hand-eye coordination. As I have said, I know that, even if I had the best tennis coach in the world, I would never really improve at that game. But running… With a bit of commitment, you will get faster, you will be able to go longer, and it will all get easier – and you will surprise not only yourself but also the people around you.

FOREVER YOUNG. It's good for you. Running is obviously good for your health and fitness – your heart, lungs, circulation and so on – but there are other physical benefits. It keeps you mobile and flexible as you get older, and, being a weight-bearing exercise, it is excellent for maintaining bone density, which is so crucial for us as we age.

There you go! I really don't think that any other activity is as convenient or cost-effective – or delivers as much bang for your buck – as running.

Now, does anyone want to buy a tennis racket – only slightly used?

How fast do you think I should progress?

"EVERYONE TALKS ABOUT this runner's high. But I certainly haven't had it yet."

"You know, about four weeks after I started, I did my usual route and halfway round I suddenly realised that for the first time, it didn't hurt. I was ecstatic."

"That hill is still as hard as it was on day one."

No two runners start from the same place, or progress at the same rate. You are an experiment of one, as they say. Just because Fred down the road is flying after three weeks, doesn't mean you should be.

So, if you've followed my advice and jogged or run for a few weeks now, what should you expect?

Firstly, the human body is amazing – yes, even yours! – and it can adapt to do things that you thought weren't possible a little while ago, given two things – enough time to change, and the right stimulation (training).

So, you have to be a bit patient. Like most things worth doing, jogging/running requires some effort over time.

Secondly, you do have to put the effort in. Despite the millions of words written about how to run (including my own!), running is a pretty uncomplicated activity. Pretty much anything you do in terms of walking, jogging and running will have an effect over time – your body **will** adapt to the stresses put on it and you **will** improve.

Thirdly, going back for a moment to 'week one' basics, do make sure you have a decent pair of shoes. Do make sure you eat and drink enough before and after you exercise, so that you have enough energy and hydration to feel good but not too full. Do make sure you start each session by walking for a few minutes. All these things will help you to achieve the progress that your effort merits.

Beyond that, what should you expect?

(There are many online guides you can use, of course, notably Couch to 5k, but, having worked with dozens of runners starting out, this is my take.)

Someone who has been jogging/running two to four times a week for six weeks should progress from, say, being able to jog for a minute before needing to stop in week one to managing to last for between five and 10 minutes in week six. They should also be able to run all the way up a not-too-steep 100-yard hill that saw them walking after 10 yards in the first week or so.

But don't expect improvement to be smooth. You will find that you will plug away for weeks without any discernible difference, and then suddenly it will all become easier – or faster – or both.

Try and be consistent. We all have difficult weeks when everything conspires against our plans, but jogging/running is a wonderfully convenient activity. Just try and get out there. Even if it's for 10 minutes.

If you are really struggling with motivation, just tell yourself that you'll walk for five minutes and if you don't feel like it after that, you'll turn round and come home. (Usually, that walk will turn into a jog, which will in turn last for longer than you expected.)

Do try and arrange to jog/run with a friend. If you've made the commitment, you're far more likely to keep it, rather than letting them down.

Do try and establish a weekly routine – steady run with a friend on Tuesday, short run on a Thursday, parkrun on Saturday morning, and a long walk on Sunday.

Do keep a simple log of what you've done. Again, you are far more likely to get out of the door when it's hard, if you can look at your diary, phone or laptop and see how far you've come. "I've done 15 sessions in six weeks, totalling about 35 miles. I can't stop now."

And for inspiration, look online – there are some great jogging/running videos that will get you going. Three of my favourites are by Salomon. Google 'Salomon Trail Dog', 'Salomon Mount Marathon' and 'Salomon Of Fells and Hills'.

If you want a great run, go loopy!

YOUR REGULAR JOGGING/RUNNING route should be like a pair of old slippers – familiar, comfortable and comforting, and just the right size and shape.

What do I mean?

In order to get out of the door on a regular basis, you've probably realised by now that you need a regular route or routes.

What should you look for when choosing one?

Well, obviously, it should be the right length for you – it could be a mile; it could be five or six miles. It all depends on where you are in your fitness journey.

It should probably start from your front door. It's nice to drive off to the woods or a park and just run there, but getting in the car is an extra obstacle, and you're more likely to actually do it on a regular basis if it starts where you live. You can always save the other locations for longer or faster runs.

Try and make it a loop, rather than out and back. With the latter, on the way out, you are always thinking, 'I've got to do all this on the way back', whereas with a loop, you feel that you are always somewhere different and are getting to explore more. It's just more satisfying, somehow.

The first bit shouldn't be too demanding. I've been running for so long now that my knees and feet complain at the start of every run, so my regular route has a lot of flat and downhill in the first mile or so. This eases me into the run, so that by the time the hills start, my joints are more cooperative!

It should be safe. There are two factors here. For obvious reasons, ladies should be wary of jogging/running in the middle of nowhere, where they could be attacked.

The other factor is traffic. There are enough quiet roads, footpaths, parks and country lanes around our lovely towns and villages, so you should be able to design a route that does not necessitate you running on the hard shoulder of the A31.

It should be pleasant. This will mean different things to different people, but whether you like leafy lanes, picturesque parks or rolling roads, try and develop a route with at least some parts to which you will look forward.

It should be right for you. Do you want a route that's dead flat, or would you be happier with something more undulating, where you are prepared to slog up the hills for the reward of coasting down the other side? And do you prefer the firmness and predictability of pavements or roads, or do you enjoy being off-road, immersing yourself in the countryside?

Lastly, be patient. It can take a while to hit upon a favourite route, and you may find you are tweaking it from time to time, as you find slight variations. This could be a result of exploration – 'that footpath comes out **there**! And then I can pick up that other route' – or your developing fitness. When you've done a bit more training, that hill that you shunned at the start is suddenly runnable, and it opens up a whole new set of possible regular routes.

I have lived in Alton for over 20 years, and only last week I discovered a new route – one that is just the right length, that is a loop from my front door, that is actually almost completely flat, that is practically traffic-free, and that links together some beautiful countryside.

So, you see, you can teach an old running dog new treks!

"I JUST CAN'T FIND THE TIME TO RUN." MORNINGS ARE YOUR TIME!

I CAN ONLY see five yards in front of me. I can only touch the leaves and the earth under my feet. I can only hear my own breathing. I can only feel my dog's warm breath on the back of my calves.

Life is reduced to the box of visibility that I inhabit, just as much as my head torch can illuminate. It's 4:20 on a Thursday morning, I am running round a field just outside Alton, and the world is mine!

It's a nice feeling.

Lots of people say to me: "I just can't find the time to run."

Well, this is my recommendation: see if you can get out first thing in the morning. It doesn't have to be 4:20am, for goodness' sake, just whatever 'first thing' is for you!

Any other time is problematic. You can tell yourself, 'I'll get out at lunchtime', and work gets in the way. You can promise yourself you'll run in the evening, but family life is all-consuming, and that meal is all too tempting, and anyway, by that time you're tired.

But in the mornings, no one can interrupt you. (I know for those of you with young families, this may take some organising, or some give and take.)

Give it a go.

Now, a word of warning, until you get used to it, running in the morning can be hard for some people. When I first started to try it, I felt like an absolute zombie. It was a struggle to put one foot in front of the other – at least for the first few minutes.

But it gets better – in two senses. On each morning run, after that first few minutes, you will start to feel better. And after a few weeks of doing one or more of your jogs or runs in the morning, you will notice you've got more used to them.

There are so many benefits to morning running – in addition to the fact that you've done it and don't have to worry about whether you'll fit it in for the rest of the day!

There is strong scientific evidence that running in the morning raises your metabolic rate, more than if you ran at another time of the day. What that means is that you will carry on burning more calories for the next day or so.

Running in the morning also lets you see the world at its freshest. It's peaceful, the air is good, there may be morning mist or even a sunrise to look at, any people who are about are usually more friendly, and there's almost certainly less traffic.

Also, running first thing makes you just feel so blooming virtuous.

But, as I've said, it can be hard, so give yourself every chance. Set the alarm, put any contact lenses or glasses that you may need within easy reach, set your kit out the night before, if you are going to eat or drink something before you run, get that as organised as it can be – even filling the kettle can help!

I wouldn't recommend eating too much because, by definition, it's not going to be long until you run – but a cup of tea or coffee and half a banana or an energy bar can help you feel more human.

Limit the amount of time you spend between getting up and getting out there. If you linger too long, then, yes, that pile of washing does need to be done, those emails do need to be sent – you'll find reasons to stop yourself going out.

Bottom line on this: establish a routine. When I was commuting to work, I used to get up, have a cup of tea, shave, pack anything I needed for the day, prepare breakfast, and then go. It was about 40 minutes – and it shouldn't be any longer than that, or you may waver in your determination to run.

Now, working from home, it is nearer 10 minutes – partly because I am used to it, but mostly because my dog won't tolerate any further delay once she knows I am up!

And, of course, certainly while you're still getting used to running in the mornings, plan yourself a short-ish, easy route.

If you can get out there – like me and my dog – relish it – the freshness, the fitness, the feeling (certainly at the finish) and the favour that you've just done yourself.

INJURIES ARE AN OCCUPATIONAL HAZARD FOR A RUNNER. WHAT CAN YOU DO ABOUT THEM?

'I CAN'T RUN. I'm injured.'

It's so frustrating – you've made the effort to get out there and run, and now you're injured and can't.

What should you do?

First thing to say: I am not a doctor. If in doubt about any injury, go and see your GP for professional advice. The thoughts below are just a summary of my experiences of more than 50 years of largely injury-free running.

Second thing to say: as runners, we hate being injured. We don't react well to it, so you're not alone in becoming grumpy when injured! We will try to run when we shouldn't, and we maybe don't run when we could!

Injuries, like runners, come in all shapes and sizes. In general, if you can still run with an injury, and the injury gets better during the course of the run, then carry on. Obviously, be sensible and don't push things by going either too fast or too far – but easy to moderate jogging or running can actually help your circulation, speed up your complete recovery and, of course, make you feel better. ('At least I'm doing something.')

If you do get injured, check your running shoes. Are they too old or too worn? Are they not giving you the support and protection you need? Some runners keep a log of how many miles they run in each pair and ditch them at about 500 miles. But you can usually see from the soles if they are past their best.

So, what are the most common running injuries?

Probably to knees, Achilles tendons, hamstrings, groins and feet.

Knee pain is usually caused by the kneecap not 'tracking' correctly. It is being pulled out of alignment because the muscles around it are too tight or too weak to maintain its correct motion. It is probably best to get professional advice about this, but usually strengthening your leg muscles – principally the thighs – and stretching will help.

I have found that a great exercise to help with your knees is wiggling your kneecap up and down by tightening and relaxing your thigh muscles. It takes a bit of practice to get the hang of this, but I think it works really well on strengthening the thigh muscles and, at the same time, promoting the correct tracking of the kneecap.

Achilles tendon pain is usually caused by your calves being too tight and pulling on the Achilles. You need to stretch your calves gently. Only do this when your muscles are warm. So, **after** a jog or vigorous walk, place the toes of one foot on a step and ease the heel towards the step below – gently. You will feel the stretch in your calf. Hold it, repeat it, and then repeat for the other leg.

You can usually continue to jog with a minor hamstring strain or tear, but be guided by the level of pain. You may simply need to rest it for a week. Use the **RICE** acronym – **R**est, **I**ce, **C**ompression, **E**levation – to promote faster recovery.

The groin is similar. You may be able to jog gently with it or you may need to rest for a while.

The most common foot injury is plantar fasciitis, which is manifested as heel pain. This can be serious and require long-term rest and treatment.

It can be relieved by the right shoes which will support the arch, which is often the cause of this injury. If you do get plantar fasciitis, and it is severe, then seek professional help.

As your running journey progresses, you will learn what you need to do to minimise the chance of getting injured, and what to do if a problem does strike. You will learn what works for you. For instance, for more minor inflammations, I have always reacted well to ibuprofen. You may be different.

Injuries are frustrating, but try not to let them get you down. Try and maintain your fitness by doing other exercise. Cycling, swimming or indoor rowing are the obvious non-weight-bearing cardio options. You may also need to modify your diet so as not to put on weight whilst you are doing less exercise.

All of this will help to keep you from being too grumpy and get you back running sooner rather than later – for which you (and your loved ones) will be extremely grateful!

AUTUMNAL BLUES? PUT ON THOSE RUNNING SHOES!

IT'S 6PM; IT'S dark; it's raining; the traffic's heavy through Alton (has that car seen me?); the path round Kings Pond is blocked; but, you know, I'm quite content jogging along and I'm actually a good deal warmer and less stressed than everybody who's struggling with uncooperative umbrellas or temporary traffic lights.

Yes, it's autumn. The clocks have gone back and suddenly we all need to rethink our running. No longer is there time after work to run in the light. Running in the dark probably dictates a change of route. Dressing for a run takes more thought than simply which t-shirt to wear. Even our commitment gets tested. Let's look at each of those challenges in turn:

TIME. When to run is now more of an issue. Of course, if you can run during the day, that's fine. Some lucky office workers with showers can run at lunchtime, though this takes discipline and for no emergencies or unforeseen deadlines to crop up in the morning. You can run first thing, when you get up, though this requires more motivation and organisation, and is generally harder physically at first. But you do feel energised – and self-righteous! – for the rest of the day. If you have to run after work, then my tip would be to get in, change and go straight out. If you stop, even just to read a few emails, you can get dragged into all that other stuff and lose the impetus to get out there. And, when running in the dark, please take sensible precautions about your route and clothing.

ROUTE. It's common sense really – and it depends on where you live. If you're in a town, there will probably be enough well-lit roads with pavements for you to get in the distance that you need. If you're out in the country, you could consider driving somewhere safer to run – a town, a track or a park with floodlights – or you'll have to plan your route very carefully to avoid things like faster roads and blind bends. Of course, you'll need to make sure that you can see and, more importantly, that motorists can see you – and that means reflective clothing, and quite probably a head torch.

CLOTHING. At this time of year, it is quite common to feel cold before a run and therefore overdress, ending up with you being boiling hot after about half a mile. Actually, you should expect to feel a bit chilly for the first few minutes. If in doubt, dress in layers that can easily be tied around your waist as you warm up. And, as I said above, don't forget the safety role that your clothing plays. Many tops, leggings and shoes now have reflective strips or panels, which are very effective in showing you up (much more so than just wearing light colours). Don't forget hats and gloves in very cold weather.

If it is icy, you may have to think twice about running. The pavements may be too slick to be safe, but, if you can find some soft ground to run round, that should be fine. Some shoes have more grip than others, but few work well on ice, whereas you can run on snow because you naturally 'dig in' on landing – though, even then, watch out for the odd icy patch.

COMMITMENT. In autumn and winter, it may not be as easy to start your run as on those balmy summer evenings, but the enjoyment should be just as great, if not greater, when you do get going – and certainly afterwards. Whereas, in the warmer months, your runs seldom see you enjoying complete isolation, winter drives more people indoors and leaves the roads and trails to you and me, the committed hardcore! Why not enjoy being the first to plant footprints in the frost or the snow? Relish being warm while others are struggling to remain so. Be proud of the fact that the weather has not stopped you.

I have talked before of David Hemery, our Olympic 400m hurdles champion from 1968. He is such an intelligent, articulate athlete, and his autobiography, *Another Hurdle*, is a masterpiece, giving real insight into the training that led to his achievements. He describes running through the Boston, Massachusetts, winter. Many athletes were using the university indoor track under an inflated, heated dome, while: "Outside on the football pitch, I was bounding through snow. Perhaps it was the psychological edge I felt, by thinking that no one else would be doing the same – given the opportunities I had."[18]

So, the route to fitness and fun – if not Olympic fame for all of us – is out there!

---

18 *Another Hurdle*, David Hemery, page 146.

WINTER RUNNING? DON'T GET COLD FEET – IT CAN BE A WONDERLAND!

"HIGHS OF JUST two or three degrees, so do wrap up warm."

"Sunset tonight will be at 3:36pm."

"…causing icy patches to form on some roads."

We all know that winter running is different, that the falling temperatures and the lack of daylight challenge our logistics, our ingenuity, our motivation – and our wardrobe!

But, let's face it, we don't live in Siberia, where a champion marathon runner once got lost in a blizzard and had to keep running hard for five hours to avoid freezing to death.

A bit of thought can certainly make winter running more feasible, more comfortable and more effective. Here are a few ideas:

ACCEPT IT'S DIFFERENT. Winter running may have to be slower. Long runs may be more difficult to complete. You may have to plan a bit more. But, accept it's different, and focus less on minutes per mile, and more on how blooming good it feels to have run in the rain and the cold.

BODY TORCHES. The light from handheld torches, and even from head torches, can bounce around, whereas that from body torches gives a more consistent and steady view of what you're running into.

COMPETITION = COMMITMENT. I advocate having a target above almost every other piece of running advice (apart from the one about scissors), and even in the depths of winter, there are a variety of road and off-road, short and long, parkrun and non-parkrun events that you can commit to, build up to and complete.

DEFENSIVE RUNNING. When you go out for a run, you expect to meet cars. When a motorist gets in their car, they do not necessarily expect to encounter a runner. Run defensively – on the pavement, or against the traffic if there is none. Stop, if necessary, or lean into the hedge to let that van pass.

ELITES LOVE CROSS-COUNTRY. The challenges of a race across the land – the hills, the mud, the uneven footing (have I sold it to you yet?) – have been behind the success of many a top performer. Sebastian Coe and Steve Ovett both raced it frequently; Steve Cram never ran an indoor race, preferring the outdoors; and Paula Radcliffe cites her 2001 World Cross-Country Championships win as her greatest race.

FROSTBITE. Best avoided, but all extremities are prey. And, gentlemen, I mean all extremities!

GLOVES ARE GREAT. Quite often, your running will keep your core and legs warm, but your hands can get very cold. Gloves are easy enough to wear and then tuck into a pocket if necessary.

HATS ARE HEAVENLY. Whilst claims that we lose 40% of our body heat through are heads are overstated, a hat can make all the difference to how you feel – especially in those first crucial minutes of a run.

INDOORS IS OK. Despite some runners' t-shirts declaring, 'Dead Before Tread', if getting on the treadmill means getting in a run that you would otherwise miss – because of icy roads, hurricane conditions, or because your thermal top's in the wash – then I'm all for it.

JET OFF. Now that we can, a winter break to run in the sun can keep the blues at bay, give us a tan to show off, and reset our running mojo. There are organised running holidays, or just jet off!

KIPCHOGE. When the weather's awful in Iten, all the tracks are muddy, and it's his turn to clean the toilets, Eliud Kipchoge, the only man ever to run a sub-two-hour marathon, just gets on with it.

LAYER UP, DON'T LATHER UP. The most obvious piece of wardrobe advice in winter is to dress in layers. We're all tempted to put too much on, so the first mile outside is less of a shock, but even if you do, then taking off the top layer and tying it around your waist, when you start to lather up, will revert you to a more comfortable temperature.

MORNING IS MINE. Family commitments allowing, you can always run in the morning. At other times, your intended outing can be blindsided by being 'Dad's taxi service' or having 'Mum's work deadline'. For a morning run, set out your kit, set your alarm – and set off.

NOON'S NOT EASY. At least it's light, but the lunchtime run can fall foul of life (see above) and requires a surprising amount of discipline. The warmth of the office or the kitchen, lingering over coffee and sandwiches, having a chat…

OTHER EXERCISE. We runners know it's just not the same, but sometimes you have to give your legs a break, and swim, or lift weights, or…or…or rest!

PRESENTS. What winter running accessory could you put on your birthday or Christmas list this year?

QUIET. When you're out on that early morning run, and it's just you and your body torch and the slight crunch of the frost under your feet, or when you're out late, after the rush hour but before closing time, just take a moment to relish the unusual quiet.

REFLECT ON THIS. Reflective strips on clothing and shoes are far more effective in getting you seen than simply wearing light colours.

STUDS STICK. If you are running off-road and it's muddy, or running on-road or pavement in the snow, then studs can be a great idea, as they 'dig in' on landing and give you the grip that you need. Don't wear them too far on tarmac as they will quickly wear out. And watch for the odd patch of ice under the snow.

T IS FOR TURN, NOT TEA. If you are running after work, then get in, change and turn straight round and go out. Once you stop to put the kettle on and start to check emails, it won't happen.

UMBRELLAS. Watch out for them and the dangers of running up behind a careless owner – they can have your eye out, you know!

VITAMINS ARE VITAL. It only makes sense to ensure that you are getting enough nutrients to support your exercise programme and help you avoid winter's more prevalent germs. I mean, avoid colds and coughs if you can. If I see someone walking towards me in the supermarket, and they are sneezing all over the place, or simply sporting a very red nose, I just turn and go the other way!

WATERPROOFS. Whatever the manufacturers claim, these layers tend to make you overheat. In my experience, unless you're out in the hills for hours, there are very few days in the UK when you really need to run in a true waterproof. If you can get through that first uncomfortable mile in a long-sleeved, breathable top, the running itself will keep you warm – even if you're wet!

XOXO. Hugs and kisses to all of you who run through the winter!

YOU. In the end, it is all about you, and if you want to run every day through winter, that's great. Alternatively, if you want to scale it back, and build up more strength in the gym, more flexibility with yoga, or more swimming and cycling so you can enter a spring triathlon, then that's your prerogative.

ZONE. Early the other morning, moon- and torch-lit around Kings Pond, sprinting for a personal best on my five-miler, I just knew that this was where I wanted to be. I was hurting but I was in control. I was in the zone. See you there!

RUNNING IN THE DARK, THE WET AND THE COLD? GET OUT OF HERE!

"THERE IS IN Boston, at Harvard University where Dave spent last winter, an incredible air-tight bubble over an indoor wooden track. Inside, in the warm air, athletes would be prancing about in shorts and singlets going through their training routines. Outside, in a temperature well below freezing – at least 12 degrees of frost – was a muffled, tracksuited David Hemery bounding through the deep snow, building his strength, physically and mentally. Occasionally he would stop at the Plexiglas® window of the dome and peer inside, into the warmth."[19]

Because of such dedication, Hemery won 1968 Olympic gold (400m hurdles, in a world-record time), 1972 silver (4 x 400m relay) and 1972 bronze (400m hurdles).

As the temperature drops, the weather gets more miserable and the days get shorter, you may be tempted to give up exercising outdoors for a while, but there are many reasons why getting out there is good for you.

You don't have to be an Olympic hopeful, searching for that psychological edge over your competitors, to reap the benefits.

Exercising outdoors does make you feel blooming virtuous, doesn't it? Everyone else is falling asleep in front of the telly, trying to keep warm

---

19 *Munich 72*, Christopher Brasher, page 49.

and dry on their commute, struggling with recalcitrant umbrellas, or peering through fogged-up windscreens.

But the wonderful resources of the human microcosm (aka, your body) ensure that you are nice and comfortable – and, what's more, you're achieving something.

With all of the 'technical' running gear available now, there is really no need to be cold or wet. On the coldest days, though, I would advocate warming up a bit indoors if you can – do some press-ups, sit-ups or squats, or run up and down the stairs – otherwise outside will feel very cold indeed, and you may succumb to the temptation to go out dressed in far too much.

Don't freeze, of course. Getting out of the door is hard enough without knowing you're going to suffer for the first few minutes – but do recognise that you will warm up pretty quickly, even if you feel a little cold at first. You can always wear an outer layer that you can tie round your waist after the first mile or so.

Running outdoors is also far better for you than pounding the treadmill: the variations of the surface force your muscles and joints to work harder to accommodate the subtle changes, conditioning your body from every angle and in every plane; and the hills, the headwinds, the grass and the mud will demand more too, making you burn more calories than on that oh-so-predictable treadmill.

Running in the natural environment – even in the dark – has also been proven to be better for your mental and emotional health. It lifts your mood.

Shorter days do mean that you are more likely to have to run in the dark, and, if so, you should take sensible safety precautions. Many modern tracksuits, jackets, leggings and running shoes have hi-vis or reflective panels, and there are very effective head torches available, as well as lights that you can clip on to your back and front. All of these will warn traffic of your presence.

You should also choose your route with the lighting conditions in mind. At night, running on lit pavements in town may be less attractive than jogging along quiet, leafy country lanes, but it is safer in suburbia. Females, in particular, for obvious reasons, should try to avoid running alone in remote locations.

We've looked at the advantages of continuing to run outside, and the differences you need to consider in winter – clothing, routes – which brings us, finally, to motivation.

Some people love running in the rain; most hate it. Some runners love the dark, when they feel they are alone in the world; for others, it's just another barrier to getting out of the door. Some embrace the cold, because they hate the really hot weather; many feel the opposite.

You can't always do much about the time of day you have to run, or the temperature and the weather you encounter, but there are lots of simple ways to make getting out of the door that bit easier.

Establish a pre-run routine. It can be as straightforward (if you're running in the morning) as get up, get dressed, ablutions, glass of water, perhaps some warm-up press-ups, out the door. But even something this obvious will have the effect of making your run more inevitable – you do this, you do that, so, of course, your run follows!

Do all you can to prepare. When I have a particularly demanding session to do the next morning, I get everything ready the night before (I sound like my Mum) – my kit is laid out (I even put my left and right socks the correct way round!), I get my contact lenses out of the box, the kettle is filled, new batteries are put in my body torch, my shoes are at the bottom of the stairs.

It may sound silly, but, as one leading supermarket says, every little helps.

It is all too easy to find reasons not to run, so I remove every possible obstacle between me and my workout.

As I said before, when it is very cold, it will help to warm up indoors – do some simple exercises, just to get the blood flowing, especially first thing in the morning. Doing the exercises will propel you into the run.

If motivation is still a problem, then try and arrange to meet someone to run with. You are much less likely to cry off a session if you are going to be letting down your running buddy by doing so.

If you can't manage that, then tell your partner or a friend of your intention to run that night or the next morning. Ask them to keep you accountable – get them to check you've done it afterwards!

Perhaps get a large piece of paper and write down all of the exercise – runs, gym sessions, swims, walking – you've done in the last 6–8 weeks (whatever will fill about half of the sheet) and pin it up somewhere. You are far less likely to stop running if you can see at a glance how far you've come – and therefore how much you would lose by giving up. Add each session to it, as you do them.

If you really can't face running, put on your kit and go out of the door. Say to yourself that you are going to jog down the road for two minutes and, if you still can't face it, you can just walk back.

That will usually end up as a decent run.

If you can't face even that, then put on your kit, get out of the door and go for a walk. This too may result in a run – and even if it doesn't, you've still done something.

In the end, it all comes down to motivation.

At the Mexico City 1968 Olympic Games, Bob Beamon broke the world long jump record by nearly two feet, winning the gold medal with the first valid effort of the competition. Lynn Davies of Great Britain, who had won the previous gold in 1964, to all intents and purposes, gave up. The Welshman said that he knew he could never in a million years jump as far as the American had. He added that, if he had thought that he could have, he would have beaten himself up for the rest of his life, because of the one night he stayed in and watched *Coronation Street* on the box, rather than going out and running up and down the sand dunes of Merthyr Mawr in the pouring rain.

Davies was criticised for his attitude, but his all-or-nothing approach had won him gold in 1964 and he wasn't in Mexico City for anything less. The title of his autobiography – *Winner Stakes All* – sums it up.

Brendan Foster won lots of races in 1975. His wife kept videos of them all. But the only one he watched, he said, while he was putting in 120 miles a week during the winter of 1975–1976, was the race he lost to Rod Dixon of New Zealand, over his best distance of 5,000m on his home track at Gateshead.

You see, he didn't want to get too pleased with himself; he didn't want to get complacent. He wanted to remind himself just how hard he had to work to prepare for the Montreal 1976 Olympic Games.

Motivation is different for everybody.

In the end, you have to try and tune in to your personal reasons for running. Is it to get fitter? Is it to lose weight? Is it to do your first 5km? Your first marathon? Is it because so-and-so said you couldn't or wouldn't? Is it because you find you can't play football with the kids for more than a few minutes without resting – and you want to change that?

Get your reason(s) front and centre of your mind – and you'll turn into the person who bounds through the snow, rather than one of the guys who spends their winter prancing about in singlet and shorts on a heated indoor track!

See you out there!

There's gold in them there hills!

MO FARAH DOES them; Eliud Kipchoge does them; Paula Radcliffe did them; Sebastian Coe did them.

If there's one type of session that will help you to improve your running speed and strength pretty quickly, it is hills.

Hills have so many advantages over most other sessions. When you haven't got access to a track, or even a nice, flat bit of road, you can almost always find a hill to run up and down.

Hills can develop your all-out speed, your speed-endurance (running faster for longer), your endurance, your leg strength and your running form all in one session.

Also, it's difficult to get injured doing hills, because you are not landing with as much force as on the flat or downhill.

So, what should your hill session look like?

As with all hard sessions, you should warm up well. This means walking a bit, then jogging easily until you are warm, then perhaps stretching the relevant muscles.

Any particular stretches?

Yes – hills will certainly test your Achilles tendons. These are the ligaments that connect your calf muscles to the bones in your feet. And they will be tested because, on hills, your heel is obviously landing below your toes.

It is not actually your Achilles getting tight that's the problem, it is the calf muscle above it, so be sure to stretch your calf muscles to prevent injury. Always stretch them when they are warm, so that means after the warm-up jog. The best way to do this is to find a curb or a step, place your toes on the higher level and ease your heels gently towards the ground below. You should feel the stretch in your calf muscles.

You should then include a few gentle strides or sprints before you start the hills themselves – 'strides' means accelerating gradually to a brisk pace that you hold for 30–40 yards before slowing down. Be sure to have a decent walk around to get your breath back and then repeat the stride 4–8 times, gradually getting faster.

Then you are ready for your hills.

Pick a hill that is not too steep. You can run on road, grass, trail – almost any surface is fine – just be sure that you can jog back down safely, that the ground isn't too slippery.

You can do short hills – 10–15 seconds – medium hills – 25–45 seconds – or long hills – 60+ seconds. They all make you work hard and they all give you slightly different benefits.

Short hills obviously give you more speed and leg strength, whilst longer efforts work speed-endurance and endurance. A mixture in one session is also good!

Start with short hills. Start your effort from an obvious landmark – a house number or a particular tree – and run as hard as you can for 10–15 seconds to another obvious point. Turn straight round and jog down, then repeat the sprint back up. Try and do four continuous efforts at first. Then maybe have a rest (walk around for two or three minutes) and repeat the four efforts.

A good session to start with is 2 x 4 fast hills. By the end of each effort, you will be glad to jog, and by the end of the four, you will be very glad to stop and walk.

All of your hills should be roughly the same speed (i.e. take the same time), perhaps getting slightly faster towards the end.

If the last one or two are much faster, then you are saving too much, and you should up the pace from the first hill. As I have shouted at my athletes many a time: "Don't save it for the last one; that's easy; anyone can do that. Put it in now and get real value from the session!"

Be disciplined with your recovery – turn round at the top and start jogging down immediately; don't be tempted to walk. And turn straight round at the bottom too and start the next effort!

That session, done properly, will have given you more speed, more leg strength, more speed-endurance and more endurance in a short space of time.

Always remember to warm down by jogging easily for 10 minutes at the end.

Longer hills will be at a slower, though still demanding, speed, and you will still be glad to stop or jog down at the top.

Eventually, you could try three short, then one long, three short, one long – all run continuously with a longer jog down immediately before and after each of the long efforts.

Doing hills in this way will also help your running form. Think about your knees coming up higher, your arms pumping a bit more vigorously, and your legs powering you more forcefully up the hill.

Speed, strength, speed-endurance, endurance and better running form – all in one handy session. Wow – no wonder Olympic champions and world record holders like Mo, Eliud, Paula and Seb do or did them. And so should you. There's gold in them there hills!

COACHES AREN'T LIKE BUSES – NOT MANY OF THE RIGHT ONES COME ALONG AT ONCE!

THE OLD MAN finished his all-out one-mile time trial and collapsed on to the infield, retching and rolling around in agony. A few minutes later, when he had finally recovered, he staggered over to the young athlete he was coaching and said something along the lines of: "You'll run many miles much faster than that, Herb, my boy, but you'll never put more effort into one."

Herb was Herb Elliott, the Australian Olympic gold medallist in the 1960 1,500m and world record holder for that distance and the mile. He remained unbeaten in his adult racing career at those events, but on this day, he was struggling for motivation.

The coach was Percy ("Pain is the purifier") Cerutty, and after that demonstration of effort, motivation was never again an issue for Elliott.

Almost every runner wants to improve, and one of the most effective things you can do to bring about improvement is to get a coach. A coach can provide the personalised advice, the experience, the perspective, the inspiration and the sheer accountability that can propel you to the next level.

But coaches are not like London buses – you don't get many of the right ones coming along at once. So, what should you look for in a coach?

COMMUNICATION. There should be regular communication – and you should be happy not only with its regularity, but also with its quality and two-way nature. It should start with an in-depth conversation about where you are, where you want to get to, what training you are doing and have done in the past, what aspects of your lifestyle affect training volume and intensity, and so on.

It should then move forward into a planning phase, a 'testing it out to see if it works' phase, and then an ongoing exchange of views. I give my athletes a schedule for 8–16 weeks; they email me every Sunday night with feedback on how it has all gone; and we talk directly if things need changing.

Interestingly, when Peter Coe was coaching his son, Sebastian, he always referred to Seb as 'my athlete' in a coaching context, never 'my son', to ensure that the communication took place with the correct level of professionalism, objectivity and respect.

ONE SIZE DOES NOT FIT ALL. If your prospective coach turns up at your first meeting and announces, "Here is your 16-week marathon training plan", then run!

Don't run the blooming schedule; run away, I mean.

Every training plan has to be as different as the individual capabilities, experiences, lifestyles and goals of its subject. I didn't give the national 100km champion the same schedule as the overweight 40-year-old Dad just starting out on his 5km journey, for instance.

Sebastian Coe and Steve Ovett were superbly well-matched athletes, swapping the world mile record by tenths of seconds in 1979–1981, but their training was very different. Peter Coe's schedule for his son was track- and gym-based, focused on speed, speed, speed. Harry Wilson's plan for Ovett was more endurance-based, with Ovett not being scared to race the odd half marathon and eventually taking Commonwealth 5,000m gold.

Your training plan should be the product of probably several lengthy conversations and a few trial weeks.

ACHIEVEMENT. Your coach should ideally have achieved a decent level of success in running themselves, in order to deliver advice, instructions, schedules and pep talks in a way that is credible to their athlete(s).

It is difficult to commit to your coach's '17-mile tempo run, with the last five all-out' when you know they've never done it themselves.

Personally speaking, I have never asked an athlete of mine to do a session that I have not done multiple times myself. I just would not feel comfortable, because, if I had not done it, I would not have understood what they were going through – and, quite rightly, they would not have fully bought into what I was asking them to do.

CUT TO THE CORE. A coach with that sort of experience will have confidence – and thus the ability to tell it like it is. Sometimes, a coach has to talk pretty straight to an athlete.

Let me repeat the tale of the national level 100km runner I advised some years ago. He was good; he was very good – he had won national medals; but he just could not break through to the next level. I looked at his schedule. It was obvious: he was doing too much. He was not giving himself any easy or rest days; the days that would allow him to run the harder days at the level he needed to, to move on.

He took my advice, toned down some of his training, and six months later he won the UK 100km championships and set a personal best.

HEART. A coach has to have a passion for running, but so does the athlete. The athlete has to have dreams – and the dedication to do the things necessary to put those dreams within reach.

Every athlete will miss sessions, or have to tone the schedule down at times, but the coach is going to get pretty frustrated if this is happening regularly. If the coach is racking their brains to define the best schedule, standing by the side of the track in all weathers, and thinking forensically about results, and the athlete's dedication does not match that commitment, then the relationship is going to be pretty short-lived.

So, get yourself a coach who will start by understanding you and giving you a personalised plan, who is happy to communicate regularly and meaningfully, who can change things around if necessary, who has reached a level of running achievement themselves, who is prepared to talk straight and not let you off the hook too many times, and whose commitment to your success matches your own.

They may not run an all-out mile for you like Percy Cerutty did for Herb Elliott, but they should be prepared to go the extra mile.

CONTEMPLATING YOUR FIRST RACE? THINK MEDALS, CAKE AND PRIDE!

"IT'S NO GOOD," said Mike Gratton to his coach, Cliff Temple, shortly before the start of the 1983 London Marathon. "I just can't do it." He wasn't despairing about the task ahead, but complaining about not being able to get the lid off his tub of Vaseline – the application of which is an important pre-race ritual for any marathoner. Mike went on to win that race in 2:09:43.

Even for elite runners like Mike, a race is not simply a case of turning up and running. If you are contemplating your first race, don't be intimidated – the rewards are well worth it. You will experience competing against your fellow human beings; you will get an exact time for a specific distance, which you can try and beat next time; you will almost certainly be offered coffee and cake at the end; you will get that bit fitter; most races will also give you a medal! And you will feel alive and proud.

But what should you be aware of in this racing lark?

First, you need to enter. Some races will have places available 'on the day', but why risk preparing for a race, driving all the way there, only to be told they're full?

Enter online and you'll be sure of your place, and it will be a couple of quid cheaper than on the day.

Mike Gratton now runs his own running events, holidays and training weeks business, 2:09 Events Limited (where did he get the idea for that name, I wonder?!), which puts on races and organises tours to foreign events and warm-weather training weeks. (I'm not on commission!)

Most running clubs will have a list of races on their website, and then there are portals such as the Runner's World site and findarace.com

The online entry systems are pretty sophisticated now. You'll probably only have to do the laborious task of entering all of your details once – and then they'll be remembered for when you enter another race.

How do you choose the right event for you? Well, go for something fairly near you, and then decide on the distance and the terrain that appeal.

Obviously, if you've only run up to five miles, don't enter a marathon! But, if you have done five miles a couple of times, then a 10km would be a good aim and give you something to train for.

Now, the terrain. Some people like the predictable footing of road; others love the scenery and challenge of the trails, where the routes tend to be more technical (think hills, bends, roots, mud, streams, logs to leap over).

Most race publicity will offer some sort of a description – 'quiet, pretty country lanes', 'flat and fast', 'severely undulating', 'awesome medal', 'mountains of cake'. See, I told you!

Once you've chosen your race, then you need to carry on preparing for it. If it is a bit further than you've run before, hopefully the race will give you motivation to get out and do a bit more running.

But whatever you do, don't overdo it in the week before the race, and in the last couple of days, be lazy. Forget your 10,000 steps. Don't be tempted to use those last days to clear the garage, rearrange the loft or have a blitz in the garden.

You'll knacker yourself for your event!

Next: food, drink and sleep. For a race up to 10km, there's really no need to eat any extra. Sorry! For 10 miles or a half marathon, you might consider having a decent amount of pasta the night before, but do eat food you are used to and that you know won't upset your stomach.

Make sure you are well hydrated – no, not with beer or wine! – and try and sleep well in the two nights prior to the event. Cut your toenails.

I know I sound like your Mum, but set your kit out the night before. You'll have enough to think about on the morning of the race, so do all you can to prepare for it in advance.

I have turned up to a cross-country race and discovered that I only had work shoes to run in! I know one ultra-runner who had to do 40 miles on the road in his shiny black business brogues! Not fun, and a recipe for back problems.

Don't wear anything for the race itself – especially shoes – that you haven't tried and tested, and 'worn in' on a few runs already. If you've been sent your number in the post, pin it to your top the night before. Take clothes to wear before the race to keep you warm, and after for when your racing gear is sweaty or muddy, or both.

If it's a cold day, to keep warm, wear an extra layer that you can discard at the last minute, or hand to a friend, or even tie round your waist after a mile or so.

Also pack drinks and energy bars, and perhaps a towel. Sunglasses, hat, gloves, watch, Garmin®?

Think about where you're going to put your car key during the race. If you haven't got a non-running friend to keep it for you, and the event doesn't offer bag storage, make sure your shorts or leggings have a zipped pocket.

Having all of this sorted out the day before will also help you relax and sleep better.

In the morning, get up in plenty of time. Depending on your preference, you may have breakfast – again, something you're used to – or you may have a different pre-run routine. Perhaps you just have a cup of coffee and a banana or an energy bar.

Make sure you know where you are going and leave with time to spare.

I like to arrive nearly an hour before my race start time – and half an hour is the minimum.

Why? Because there is likely to be a bit of a walk from the car park to the start; because you'll probably want to visit the toilet at least once; because you may want to warm up a bit; because you may need to find where to store your bag; and because you don't want to just leap out of the car and run!

Having mentioned warming up, it is something I would recommend for any race. There is a saying, the shorter the race, the longer the warm-up.

You're nervous and it is probably the last thing you want to do, but even jogging around for a few minutes, plus a few stretches or drills, can get you physically – and mentally – better tuned up for the race. Double-knot your shoes.

If it is up to you where in the 'pack' to line up, be sensible. If you are unlikely to beat the hour for this 10km, don't stand at the front. You'll just get barged and trampled, and you certainly won't enjoy the first few hundred yards.

Many races have signs along the start funnel with predicted times on them. And, as most races are chip-timed now, you don't lose anything by standing back from the actual start line. This is because the race system reads your chip as you pass over the start, and again at the finish, giving you your actual running time for the advertised distance.

Your first race will naturally be a learning experience, but, when it comes to pace, try not to get excited and go off too fast. That would make the second half of the race a pretty painful experience.

Such is the sophistication of modern digital devices that you will probably have all of the data you need from the start, so you can fine-tune your pace as you go. But try and use your running instinct to tune into how you feel.

In some senses, the race itself is the easy – or at least – the simple, bit. There will probably come a time in the middle where you are far enough in for it to be hurting, but not so far that you can see the finish. That is the time to believe in your training and to focus in on exactly how tired you are, how fast you are running, and how far you have to go. (Could you go faster? Should you slow down?)

Keep the belief and grit it out until you are near enough to the finish to gauge what you've got left, and go for it if you can.

And then, it's all over. You cross the finish line, stagger onward to the medals and the goody bags, grab a cup of water and a banana, and start to feel proud. Now, where's that cake?

And for the rest of that day – and the days to come – that feeling of pride will grow and deepen. You will savour the ache in your legs. You will enjoy your post-race beverages and food even more than normal. And you won't want to take that medal off!

Good luck!

If you've laboured through this Beginners' Section – and indeed laboured through your running apprenticeship – you may be interested in some of the stories, ideas and thoughts elsewhere in the book. Something could propel you towards an even more exciting running future. I wish you all the very best.

ACKNOWLEDGEMENTS

RUNNING HAS BEEN a major part of my life for more than 50 years, so naturally very many people have helped me in that time. If I've forgotten anybody, my apologies – it's been a long time and a lot of brain cells can come loose in half a century.

My late father first talked to me about running, specifically about watching Sydney Wooderson win handicap track races, sometimes setting world records, at Motspur Park or Tooting Bec before the Second World War.

When I started serious competition, it was in race walking, and Keith Read, Peter Selby, Nolan Simmons, Roger Lancefield, Ray Hague and Roy Posner all coached, supported or trained with me. Before I could drive, Peter would ferry me to races as far afield as Bradford, and then support me from the roadside – "If you look behind you now, you'll get a lovely view of Ilkley Moor."

Moving on to running, the good folk at Basingstoke and Mid Hants AC have always supported me, notably Ken and Wendy Littlejohns, Ian Byett, Terry Wegg, Andy Cullen, Tom and Paula Steckiw, Wally 'the Thorpedo' Thorpe, Tim Fowler and Don Powell.

The GB Ultra squad, of course, provided assistance at many levels, notably from John Legge and Tony Jones, and inspiration from rubbing shoulders with the likes of Don Ritchie, James Zarei, Eleanor Robinson, Hilary Walker and Steve Moore, each of whom has far more right to pen their story than I have. Don's book, *The Stubborn Scotsman*, is a masterpiece, and I was honoured to get a mention in it.

I almost literally bumped into Paul Nihill, Olympic silver medallist in the 50km walk in 1964, more than once, training around the streets of South London in the 1970s and he also gave me valuable advice in the lead-up to the Quadrathon in 1983 and 1984, where he was manager of the race walk stage.

Latterly, Alice Holt parkrun has been a major focus for me, and I am grateful to so many people there for their hard work, their volunteering and simply their companionship in making this event so great – a home from home for me – Martin Bushell, Paula Patterson, Geoff and Kathy Brown, Craig Tate-Grimes, Andy Clegg, Dan Davies, Debbie and Nick Whitehead, Carolyn Wickham, Justin Clarke, Terry Copeland, David Bateman, Rachel Morris, Alison Kemp, Douglas Blyth and Nick Whishaw.

Runners I have coached have always been a source of inspiration for me. There have been many over the years, but perhaps Sue Cullum, Laura Cullum and Caroline Rixon have lasted the longest!

Closer to home, I have run many a mile with family dogs, Junga (9,563.5 miles) and Roni (16,276.5 miles) – both far more reliable than any human training partner.

Over the years, I have also run countless miles with the likes of Ian Fletcher, Mick Dunne, Chris Hibberd, Warren Beese ("we'll just run to the office"), Giles Peckham and Phil Pascoe.

I have been on more mad running (and cycling) adventures with Paul 'Thommo' Thompson than with anyone else, during which he has shown an admirable consistency in completely overestimating his own abilities, going off too fast, somehow managing to crawl to the finish, and later falling asleep **in** his curry. "I only made one mistake – I thought I was fit." Gobble, gobble, mate, one more run!

This book is dedicated to Rod Lock, with whom I have run many miles, but more importantly from whom I have received endless hours of support on the roadside – "A cup of water held by a friend / Is worth more than any cup won at the end." Mick Varley was along on many of our joint trips to Paris, New York City and South Wales! I'll just say, "English equipment", "Combien", "Excuse me, Sir, you're short", "Another great lap" and "La grande mousse"!

I would like to thank Mike Gratton, 1983 London Marathon winner and founder of 2:09 Events Limited, for writing the Foreword.

I would also like to thank Steph Tranter of Steph Tranter – Be more you! for starting to make me believe, way back in 2016, that I was worth a book, so to speak. It's been a long road, Steph!

I am also extremely grateful to the Herald group of newspapers (published by Tindle Newspapers Surrey & Hampshire Limited) in the shape of Colin Channon, Editorial Manager, and Daniel Gee, Head of Content, who gave me the opportunity to test out my writing skills in a running column.

The actual production of this book would probably not have happened – and certainly would have been a lot less fun – without the prompting of the Accountability Group, namely Jonathan Howkins, Matthew and Jenny Burch, Mark Alcock, Mark Eastlake, Anna Hodges and Dominic Tantram. Sam Pearce of SWATT Books and Craig Smith of CRS Editorial have also worked wonders in transforming the material from a simple Word document to the book you are holding.

Other friends who, directly or indirectly, have encouraged me to tell my story along the way include Brian and Bridget Nash, Colin Selby, Phil Avery, Mandy Bennett, Vicky and Beth Allott-Hales, Lynne Wardale, Keith Godfrey, Jim Culverwell, Jeanne Perrett, Hannah Mantle, Mark and Jan Thompson, Gemma and Gareth Allen, James "Bearface" Wood, Neil Kelso, Dr. Sharief Ibrahim, James White, Robyn Bowyer, Ian Linsley, Melissa Simm, Sally Titmus, Alan Pryce, Glyn Hibberd, Jane Carley and Rachel Adams.

Mel, maybe you're right – maybe "it was my fate from birth to make my mark upon the earth".

Beverley Nash Pryce has remained a constant source of support for more than 35 years.

And finally, my children, Harry and Gabriella, who unfortunately failed to dodge the running/exercise gene, and who remain a source of joy, support and inspiration for the old man.